Rapha's Handbook *for* Group Leaders

Rapha's Handbook *for* Group Leaders

Richard Price
Pat Springle
and
Joe Kloba

Rapha Publishing
Houston, TX

Rapha's Handbook for Group Leaders
by Richard Price, Pat Springle, and Joe Kloba
Copyright © Rapha Publishing, 1991. All rights reserved. No portion of this book may be used in any form without the written permission of the publisher, with the exception of brief excerpts in magazine articles, reviews, etc.

Scripture quotations are from the New International Version, Copyright © The International Bible Society 1973, 1978, 1983.

First Printing, 1990
ISBN: 0-945276-31-1
Printed in the United States of America

CONTENTS

PART I: *THE GROUP ENVIRONMENT*
1

THE GOALS AND PURPOSES OF A GROUP 3

2

THE MECHANICS OF A GROUP DISCUSSION 13

PART II: THE MEMBER'S GROWTH

6

7

8

APPENDIX

ACKNOWLEDGMENTS

Thanks to Sandy Ballard, Kerry Edwards, Sharlene Johnson, and Robert Pace for their contributions to this material.

INTRODUCTION

God has used small groups throughout history to influence people's lives. We see this most clearly in the ministry of Jesus Christ. Even though He ministered to the masses, He also sought to develop the faith of the twelve disciples in the context of a small group. After His earthly ministry, Jesus' early followers continued this use of small groups. For example, Paul trained small groups of leaders as he founded churches throughout Asia Minor and Greece.

After the establishment of Christianity, God has continued to use the small group context to effect change in His people's lives. In England, for example, John Wesley established a renewal movement through his use of "societies" and "bands," small groups of people formed to sustain personal Christian growth.

Today, the need for effective small groups has increased. Our mobile, urban society creates a longing in people to belong. People who move, on average, once every two to three years and whose extended families are separated by hundreds of miles possess a need to be involved significantly with other people. They need the support of others who care for them; they need to belong to a group of people who knows and loves them.

Modern society and God's historical use of the small group format provide ample justification for your desire to be an effective small group leader. Leading others in a discovery of God's truth and what it can mean for their lives is an exciting opportunity. Yet, in the words of one experienced group leader, the new leader often experiences "self-doubt, anxiety, and downright trepidation." *Rapha's Handbook for Group Leaders* is designed to help you overcome these roadblocks so that you will feel comfortable, equipped, and adequate for the job of leading a group of people in this discovery.

Meeting the "felt" needs of people

As explained more fully in Chapter One, this handbook provides resources for leaders of growth and support groups. These groups focus upon the emotional, relational, and spiritual needs of people. People attend growth and support groups because the groups speak to their felt needs. The circumstances of their lives may have produced hurt, anger, loss, disappointment, or abuse. Some encounter circumstances which result from their misguided choices. Others experience the effects of other people's irresponsibilty. All are seeking solutions and hope. As a result, we expect that you will deal with people's feelings during the course of your small group.

Many people are wary of starting groups in their churches which deal with people's emotional issues. One newcomer to a growth group commented, "We ought to be dealing exclusively with God's Word and drop this attention on family background and emotions. We're just selling out to the world." Indeed, many growth groups over the years have given little attention to biblical guidance and have encouraged a drift away from the Word of God. In these cases, suspicion is justified.

However, when biblical content is applied to people's emotional lives, this concern subsides. Many Christians believe that our knowledge of and belief in the truth is the only thing that should influence our behavior. In reality, what we feel influences what we do almost as much as what we believe. Christianity is not simply a matter of thinking and doing. Nor should we merely feel and do. Rather, we should think, feel, and do. For example, if we emotionally experience the love of God in addition to mentally believing in His love, we will act in ways that demonstrate the truth that God is loving. David confessed, "Surely you [God] desire truth in the inner parts; you teach me wisdom in the inmost place" (Psalm 51:6).

These "inner parts" include what we call our emotions. When handled in this fashion, the discussion of emotional issues should actually be welcomed.

One pastor voiced deep disappointment over his life and ministry. He recalled his initial calling to ministry and described how those early dreams had not come true. He said, "I know God causes all things to work together for good for me. I know He cares for me. I just don't feel it." He was experiencing a conflict between what he knew to be true and what he felt to be true. Admirably, he still chose to believe in God's loving concern for him. Yet, in the depths of his heart, he lacked the assurance that God really cared, and his behavior showed it. He represents thousands of people who will benefit from dealing with difficult circumstances from a biblical perspective.

The information found in this handbook will help you begin to lead others in applying God's truth to the deepest parts of their lives. It will not train you to be a counselor. Nor do we demand you become one. In fact, you may encounter situations when you need to refer a group member to someone trained in professional counseling. Yet, you will find insights into why people believe one thing and do another in spite of their beliefs, and you will discover ways to help them live more genuinely.

Small groups in the church

We believe the small groups which function in a local church should do so under the leadership of that church. In many churches, the leadership already has a policy which guides the nature and growth of the church's small group ministry. As a result, we encourage those who want to start a small group to approach their church's small group coordinator or their pastor about their desire.

This handbook and our materials do not depend upon any particular guiding policy for church small group ministries. The only natural condition is that the church leadership recognize the need to minister to people's personal, emotional, relational, and spiritual needs in the context of small groups. Thus, this manual does not focus upon broad strategies or ways to start and organize a small group ministry in your church. Rather, it seeks to provide guidance on how to lead or facilitate an effective small group regardless of the broader policy.

In cases when a church does not have a guiding policy in place and would like to develop one, we suggest the training provided by Serendipity House (Littleton, Colorado). In his *Training Manual for Groups*, Lyman Coleman describes 15 models of successful small groups currently in use by a variety of churches. He further provides suggestions for developing a small group ministry and an annotated bibliography by Dr. Roberta Hestenes.

How to use this book

This handbook is divided into two parts. If you are a new, or even an experienced, group leader, most of what you need is found in Part I: The Group Environment. It covers all the basics. Part II: The Member's Growth contains information condensed from the counseling profession. Included here are insights into personal behavior and family systems. Whereas Part I focuses upon the group, Part II focuses upon the individual members and their hearts and healing. Although Part II contains some material excerpted from other Rapha publications, new material is included as well.

Chapter One focuses upon the purposes and varieties of small groups found in the local church. It also contains a checklist for starting your small group. Chapter Two contains the "nuts and bolts" of running a small group. We give suggested formats, ground rules, and a weekly check list. In addition, we cover tips on managing difficulties which naturally arise, along with guidance on asking good discussion questions. In Chapter Three we turn our focus to the less tangible aspects of small group leading. These include the elements of a successful small group, the dynamics of group leadership, stages of a small group's life, and reasons why people lead and join a small group. One particular type of support group, a 12-Step group, deserves special attention. In Chapter Four we describe the unique nature of a 12-Step program for overcoming addictive behaviors. We end Part I with a discussion of the ministry of your group as reflection of the family of God in Chapter Five.

Part II begins with Chapter Six. Here we explore more fully the effects families have upon their children and their adult lives. In Chapter Seven we discuss the process one goes through in the healing of emotional wounds. We continue to focus upon the process of healthy living in Chapter Eight as we discuss how to gain a practical grasp of the healing process.

We want this handbook to be practical. So we have gathered answers to the most commonly asked questions in the last section, "Questions Group Leaders Ask . . . . " Many of the answers will refer you back to sections of the book which will give you added insight and perspective. At the end of each chapter, we provide a chance for you to evaluate yourself and your situation in light of the ideas presented. If you are using this handbook to teach others how to lead small groups, please copy these evaluation questions for use in your training group. It will provide your people an opportunity to assimilate the concepts into their new role as a leader.

Rapha Hospital Treatment Centers constantly provides new resources for small group leaders. We also have available an audio tape series which complements this handbook. For a copy of an up-to-date list of our materials and prices, please call 1-800-383-HOPE and ask for Customer Service.

Quick Start

If you are interested in gaining a quick overview of the basic steps for starting a group, turn to the section "How to Get Started" on page 8 for a week by week checklist. It will point you to discussions in the rest of the book which you may need to review as you complete each step. Otherwise, each chapter can be read on its own.

PART I
THE GROUP ENVIRONMENT

THE GOALS AND PURPOSES OF A GROUP

Objectives:
- to provide an understanding of what purpose and goals you should pursue in leading a small group;
- to suggest various formats within a church in which a small group can function; and
- to guide you in the steps to take in starting your small group.

Small groups are part of the fabric of our everyday lives. Many of us car pool, eat meals, work, study, and socialize in small groups. Some groups are formal, others are informal, some are binding and permanent, others are flexible and temporary. Few of us are untouched by small groups.

Rarely do we consider the purpose and goals of these groups. Yet, they function quite well. They succeed largely because they are such a familiar part of our lives. We enter meetings at work knowing the purpose is to accomplish a certain task. We attend parties with the understanding that the goal is to have fun.

It is not always necessary to discuss the rationale for a group for that group to succeed. On the other hand, a clear understanding of a group's reason for existence can greatly enhance its effectiveness. This is especially true when people encounter a new kind of group, either as a leader or as a member. Knowledge of a group's purpose enables the people involved to adjust their expectations and behavior. Without this knowledge, the group may lack cohesiveness and direction.

Types of Small Groups

Several types of small groups are found within a local church. Perhaps the most familiar are the *task groups*. These exist to accomplish a certain project whether it is organizing a retreat, selecting new church furnishings, or planning a worship service. *Teaching groups* communicate knowledge and information largely through the lecture method of instruction. Most youth classes and almost all adult Sunday School classes and education programs fit into this type of group.

Many successful churches are incorporating two additional types of groups in their ministries. First, *growth groups* are created to encourage and challenge members to grow in their personal, relational, and spiritual lives. They tend to focus upon a program of content which encourages them to grow in areas such as marriage, family and work life, Bible mastery, discipleship, self-esteem, codependency, community outreach, or social justice.

Second, progressive churches are also starting *support groups* which focus upon specific emotional or relational needs. Generally, members attend because they feel stress in coping with life's problems. People attend because they need support and perspective in dealing, for example, with grief, job loss, divorce recovery, alcohol or drug abuse, or single parenting. Support groups are generally led by *facilitators* instead of *leaders*, whose job is to promote mutual help and support.*

Each of these groups serves a useful function in the life of the church. Yet, they must be used appropriately. For example, those who are assigned the task of maintaining the church property would

(*See Dilbert, Michael and Wiehern, Frank, *Growth Groups*, Grand Rapids, Zondervan: 1985 for a slightly different approach to the differences between groups offered in churches.)

be poorly advised to select anything other than a task group approach. The types of groups employed must meet the existing needs.

One helpful way to understand the similarities and differences between these groups is to examine them in light of four major activities of groups. For example, teaching groups engage in the dispensing of information and task groups devote most of their time to planning action or actually working on projects. The following chart summarizes these activities.

ACTIVITY	FOCUSES ON	EXAMPLES
giving information	what you should know	public lectures, Sunday School classes
encouraging discussion	what you think	home Bible studies, town meetings
facilitating process	what you feel	counseling groups, grief support groups
planning action	what you do	committee meetings, workshops

The following chart describes the four types of groups in light of these four activities.

Activities	Types of Groups			
	Ministry Task	Study Teaching	Discipleship Growth	Sharing Support
giving information	medium	high	low	low
encouraging discussion	medium	low	high	high
facilitating process	none	none	medium	high
planning action	high	low	medium	medium

For example, a teaching group will be high on communicating information, low on discussion and action, and give very little or no attention to processing how the members feel about the information.

On the other hand, support groups give just enough information to facilitate high degrees of discussion and process. The primary place for action lies in the everyday lives of the members, not in the group meeting itself.

This handbook is written primarily to help you become more effective in leading a growth or support group. It will also help you conduct a teaching group with more discussion and group interaction. As mentioned in the introduction, many people, Christians and non-Christians alike, need the environment provided by growth and support groups. This is largely due to the erosion of social and family support networks in America's mobile society. The church stands in a unique position to provide light and hope to people in our society who encounter life's difficulties.

Objectives For Growth and Support Groups

Broadly speaking, growth and support groups should seek to provide an environment in which God can change lives. This objective applies to each topic for which Rapha offers materials. In addition to this broad objective, each group topic will chart its own specific objectives. These narrower objectives define more specifically the ways in which people can change. Whatever the specific objectives may be, every activity, every discussion, and every interaction should provide God with an opportunity to change people.

Through His Word we know the direction in which God wants to change His people. Yet, you will not see Him change everybody to the same degree and in the same way. Some people will change dramatically during the course of your group. Others will change in small ways. Still others may not change at all. Yet, their growth is not your responsibility. The responsibility for growth lies with God. You simply provide the nurturing environment in which God can cause growth to occur (I Corinthians 3:5-9).

Use of Rapha's Small Groups

Many people have used Rapha's growth and support group materials in already existing large group functions such as Sunday School classes, evening church training programs, and women's ministry programs. While these traditional activities generally follow a lecture style, many have found the transition to a discussion format well-received by the people in their groups. In addition, our materials provide lesson plans for 13 group discussions, so they easily fit into the quarterly programing of the church.

You can use Rapha's materials with a group which traditionally has been a teaching group by making a few modifications. This handbook is designed for use in growth and support groups. Yet, certain techniques of a small group leadership can be applied in a teaching group. For example, by using the material on effective discussion questions (found in Chapter Two), you can increase the amount and quality of class discussion and, thus, improve your class's understanding and application of the content.

Your church may already have several small groups functioning. Rapha's materials are a natural fit in these situations. For example, you may belong to a small group Bible study discussion that meets on Tuesday evenings. You could study the doctrines of salvation and how they relate to one's self-esteem (via *The Search for Significance*) during the Fall, and return to a study of Colossians in the Spring.

You may also want to start a group from the ground up. Often, people want to get to know others in the church outside the already existing programs. They may desire a more relaxed atmosphere and more time to talk with people and share their struggles, experiences, and insights. Because our material encourages personal interaction in addition to biblical input, these people can find the place where they can get to know others on a more intimate and personal level.

How to Get Started

Pray throughout the steps outlined below. You will be working hard to insure an effective group. Yet, God must work in people's hearts. You must not trust in your own efforts but in God's involvement. Pray that He will guide your decisions and change people's hearts.

Week One - *Planning the Group*

❏ Meet with your pastor or church small group coordinator to review the group and to determine your role in it. A good way to do this is to review together the following small group leader criteria:
- desire for ministry with people dealing with the issues upon which the group will focus;
- personal experience in dealing with the issues upon which the group will focus (this is especially true for those who desire to facilitate a support group);
- personal experience in small group ministry and/or completion of a group leader's training program;
- spiritual maturity and a willingness to submit to the leadership of the church staff;
- teachable spirit;
- ability to provide elements of a successful group (see pages 46-52); and
- Qualities/skills of a group leader (see pages 52-56).

❏ Identify potential co-leaders (see page 34) as well as any other individuals who might be interested in joining the group.

❏ Determine the topic for the group.

❏ Determine whether the group will be open or closed (see pages 33-34 and 62).

❏ Determine when the group will start and when and where it will meet. Keep in mind the elements in Setting the Stage (see pages 29-35).

❏ Develop a strategy for publicizing the ministry to the church.

❏ Order the materials needed. Refer to the Rapha Small Groups Brochure (or call Rapha Customer Service at 1-800-383-HOPE).

Week Two - *Publicizing the Group*
❑ Place an announcement in the church bulletin (see the descriptions of the small groups available from Rapha in our Small Groups brochure/order form; to obtain a copy call Customer Service).
❑ Make an announcement from the pulpit. If possible, include a brief testimony by the group leader. His comments should identify the features and benefits of the small group.
❑ Plan at least one announcement as a bulletin insert. Include a description of the group and the date, time, and place of the first meeting. Also, note if child care is provided and include a form for people to sign up. List the group leader's name and phone number for further information.
❑ Church-wide events can be scheduled to develop greater congregational awareness. Possibilities include:
  • a showing of *The Search for Significance* video series (this four-part series explores how we can base our self-worth upon the love, forgiveness, and acceptance of Jesus Christ, rather than upon our success and ability to please others);
  • a panel discussion on the topic of the group during a Sunday evening program; or
  • a sermon relating to small group ministry in general or to the specific topic of the group.

Week Three - *Contacting Interested Individuals*
❑ Contact (either in person or by phone, never through the mail) individuals who respond to announcements about the small group.
❑ Begin to develop a list of individuals to be involved in your core group. Based upon your situation, it is wise to have two to three individuals who meet the same criteria for group leadership listed above.
❑ Determine if anyone in your group needs child care. Either arrange for child care at the church nursery, or put together a list of reliable baby sitters for members to call and arrange their own child care.
❑ Visit the location for the group to plan the seating, temperature, and lighting. You may need to set up signs directing people to the room or house you will use.

❏ Prepare for your first meeting. See the worksheet included in Chapter Two (see pages 21-23).

Week Four - *Begin Your Group*

❏ Arrive early for your group to arrange the seating, temperature, and lighting. Also, set up any refreshments and music.

❏ Call anyone who did not attend but who said they would like to. Encourage them, letting them know that you think the members of the group would enjoy getting to know them.

❏ Your group may start small. As the word spreads, however, additional people will want to attend. View the initial group as an opportunity to learn and make necessary adjustments. Plan to add other groups as the leadership becomes available.

Evaluation Questions

1. Think back on the groups of which you have been a member in the past. What types of groups were they? What purposes do you think the group leader had for the group?

   Use the chart below and describe these groups. For example, your most recent group may have been a missions group which was high on giving content, low on encouraging discussion and process, and medium on planning action.

Name of Recent Group:	*Missions Committee*		
Giving information:	*high*		
Encouraging discussion:	*low*		
Facilitating process:*	*low*		
Planning action:	*medium*		

   * Remember: process refers to working through the why's, how's, when's, and what's of emotions.

   Alternately, think back on the groups of which you have *led* in the past. What types of groups were they? What objectives did you set for the group? Did you meet your objectives? Why or why not?

2. Read I Corinthians 3:5-9. What is your resonsibility as you lead your group?

What is God's responsibility?

How does this affect your confidence in leading the group? Does it increase or decrease your stress? Why?

3. Many new group leaders are anxious about leading their first group. Others are even terrified. What feelings do you have about leading your next group? Describe what makes you feel this way.

2

THE MECHANICS OF A
GROUP DISCUSSION

Objectives:
- to provide you with the tools needed to prepare your group discussions;
- to give suggestions for dealing with potential difficulties; and
- to provide practical tips for successful groups.

Effective groups depend upon three major factors: the character of the group leader, the group skills developed by the leader, and the amount of attention given to the practical aspects of group leading. In this chapter, we will focus upon the practical nuts and bolts of leading an effective group. We will cover the group leader's character and skills in Chapter Three.

The success of your group will depend in part upon the quality of your preparation. The time spent each week in preparation will vary depending upon your experience. Initially, your preparation will take an hour or two of your time. After you gain experience and feel more comfortable in your role, this investment of time will decrease.*

---

* For additional discussion of practical group leading suggestions for the local church, see *How To Lead Small Group Bible Studies*, Colorado Springs: NavPress, 1982 and *Small Group Leader's Handbook*, Downers Grove, IL: InterVarsity Press.

Selecting Your Objectives

You can increase the quality of your preparation by first gaining a broad perspective of the meeting. As you review the content for each week, ask yourself, "What do I want to accomplish with this content?" You can narrow the scope of this question by focusing upon the answers to three other questions: what do you want your group members to *know*, what do you want them to *feel*, and what do you want them to *do*. The answers to these questions should be fairly short and easily remembered.

What they should know: If you are using a book (the Bible or other book) as the basis of the group, you will need to select the key idea for the week's discussion. Often leaders select too many ideas to discuss or cover and the group consequently lacks focus, often running overtime. Select one main idea, at the most two, upon which to focus.

What they should feel: Ideas affect the way people think. Less obvious, but just as vital, is the concept that ideas also affect the way people feel. Many Christians are suspect of feelings because they are often contrary to the truth of God's Word. While feelings are never an adequate basis for authentic Christian living and while one should never encourage an emotionalism deficient in truth, emotions often reflect what we truly believe.

The biblical writers, especially the Hebrew poets, call upon the people of God to experience the truth of God. For example, David encourages his readers, "Taste and see that the Lord is good" (Ps. 34:8). Many Christians acknowledge that God is good; yet, few experience that goodness on an emotional level. As a result, they endure a dissonance between what they know and what they feel. In moments of brutal honesty, as in response to significant adversity or loss, they will often say that they really do not believe in God's goodness even though they desperately want to. By selecting an affective (emotional) objective for the meeting, you can help your group members bridge the gap between what they know to be true and what they feel.

What they should do: Truth calls for action. Yet, many Christians behave no differently than the non-Christians around them. They are frequently as proud, spiteful, angry, manipulative, hopeless, and self-serving as those who do not know God. By encouraging your group to consider specific behavioral goals, group members will be motivated to live out what they say they believe.

Behavioral goals should never be viewed as absolutes. In other words, do not confuse the application of truth with the truth itself. For example, giving $100 to a mission for the homeless is a legitimate application (among hundreds of other possible applications) of the command to do good to all people (Gal. 6:9-10). Yet, to claim, "God is telling you to give $100 to the homeless," is to confuse an application of the truth with the truth itself. Group members should have the freedom to refuse your behavioral goals in favor of goals they select for themselves.

One practical way to grasp your objectives for the week is to think through the implications of the content. This allows you to anticipate the group members' responses as well as to suggest more significant applications. One way to think through the implications of the content is to ask yourself, "How would I respond to that point in a group? How would I feel? What would I want to do? What practical difference does it make?"

You will have time to think through implications if you prepare a week ahead of time. For example, on Wednesday begin reading the material for the next meeting on the following Tuesday. As you go through the week you will think of questions your members might have and ways to apply the concepts in everyday life.

Meeting Format

After you have a broad perspective of the objectives for the week, you can then fit your objectives into a specific plan of action. Many effective group leaders follow, at least loosely, a consistent format each week. The following format promotes natural interaction and has been used successfully by many leaders.

This format can be modified if you wish. Many successful groups switch the discussion and prayer time (the order then is mixing, opening, discussion, prayer, and closing). This modified format allows you to spend more time praying for one another's needs (be sure to set a time limit on the discussion).

Mixing. As people arrive, help them feel welcome and at home. You might have some soft (but not melancholy) music playing in the background. Select music which is received well by the people in your group. For example, younger people in their thirties and early forties enjoy contemporary Christian music. Other styles of music should be used with other age groups.

You might provide light snacks and/or offer them something to drink (coffee, hot chocolate, soft drinks, or tea). People seem to relax when they have something in their hand. But be sensitive to people's concern for weight control. For example, you can serve both sweets and fruit, or alternate them each week.

Encourage people to talk with one another by including others in your conversations with people. You can ask about their week, work, and kids. Try to avoid mere chitchat, but realize that casual conversation can serve a purpose in warming up people to more meaningful conversation.

Opening. Gather people together, welcome everyone, and acknowledge any newcomers. Cover any group business, but avoid setting the tone of a business meeting. Simply say something like, "There are a couple of things that you may want to know about...." Also, review the group guidelines at this time (see pages 21, 24, and 32 for more on ground rules).

Sharing. Many groups will benefit if people have a chance to tell what's going on in their lives. This allows for people to begin to get to know one another. It also provides an opportunity for a person to feel he is known by others as he tells of his life.

In the early stages of a group's growth (see Chapter Three, The Dynamics of a Group), you should provide some additional guidance besides, "How are things going with you all?" When people first join a group, they are often hesitant to tell others much about themselves. They may not trust the group members yet or simply may not know how much disclosure is expected.

For the first few weeks you might begin by asking questions similar to the following:

"Tell us where you're from."

"Tell us where you work and what kind of work you do."

"Tell us how you met your wife (or husband)."

"Tell us the two best things your family did when you were growing up."

Later, as the members of the group have grown in their trust for one another, you can ask questions like, "What was the high point and the low point of your week?"

Be sure to affirm people's contributions and avoid sarcastic or critical remarks like the plague (these kinds of remarks are often cloaked in humor).

Prayer. A simple opening prayer by you or someone else in the group is appropriate for a group of Christians. Later, when the members know and feel comfortable with one another, you can spend more time praying for group requests.

Discussion. The bulk of your group time will be spent in discussion of the topic for the week. The flow of the discussion can be traced through the following steps.

• *Hook.* Begin the topic for the evening by raising their interest in the discussion. In this "hook" you are usually setting up some sort of tension, not between group members, but between competing ideas or concepts (which is true?) or between a good idea and its application (is it practical?). This tension propels the group's discussion forward; and when it is resolved, the discussion is over.

For example, to "hook" a group into a discussion of God's love you must first narrow the topic. What about God's love do you wish to explore? Let us say you choose to focus upon the enduring character of God's love even when we sin. You can "hook" their interest in the discussion by explaining a hypothetical story of a young Christian girl who has gotten an abortion. She is concerned that God does not love her anymore.

Then ask, "What would you say to this girl about God's love?" Most Christians in your group will say something like, "Of course, God still loves you." If you leave the issue there, the discussion pretty much ends.

But if you say something like, "But what if the girl tells you, 'You don't understand! I told God to go to hell! I was going to do what I wanted and what He thought didn't matter.'" Some in your group will be stumped; they will be "hooked" into the discussion as they seek an answer to your question.

Others will attempt to resolve the tension by responding with something like, "Of course, God still loves you, if you say you're sorry." Tension resolves and the discussion faces a premature close. Again, add more information about this girl by saying, "But this girl doesn't want to say, 'Sorry.' She still believes she was right, God was wrong. But she wants God's love. What would you say to her then?" You've reintroduced tension around the issue, "Is there a practical limit to God's love?" and still others are "hooked" into the discussion.

• *Exploration.* After you have raised the group's interest in the topic for the week, you will guide the group's discovery of the issues through your discussion questions. The key word here is "guide."

Consider the role of a trail guide for a horseback trip in the mountains. He knows where to go and how to get there. Yet, he involves the tour group in the process of setting up camp, packing the horses, and preparing the meals. He knows when the trail opens into a beautiful valley and allows the group to precede him into the meadow. As a result, the people on the trip feel a sense of discovery and awe.

Your role as a guide is similar. You know where the group members need to go in their understanding and development. Yet, they need to discover these goals themselves. Your major tools are not horses and campsites, but good discussion questions. With them, you guide your group down the path of discovery.

On the practical side, if you are not using a study guide, you will need, first, to construct an outline of the topic and, second, to develop a series of good discussion questions. This takes a fair amount of experience to do well. If, on the other hand, you are using a study guide, such as one of Rapha's *Small Group Leader's Guides* which corresponds to our books, much of this work is already done for you. Even so, you may still need to come up with a few additional discussion questions to guide the discussion (see pages 28-29 on asking good questions).

• *Application*. Ultimately, the tension over competing ideas (in our example, God's limited love vs. God's boundless love) will be resolved. You should, however, reintroduce the tension and keep the discussion going by focusing upon their application of the prevailing idea.

You can ask, "In what situations do you feel God withholds a portion of His love from you?" In this way, you focus the group's attention upon the application of the truth or insight into their lives.

Applications can be cognitive (what a person thinks), affective (what a person feels), or behavioral (what a person does). No single application should be forced upon every person. Rather, each group member should select applications which are appropriate for his or her own situation.

Closing. You should signal the end of the discussion and close the meeting. If the discussion has led to some resolution of the issues, you can simply say, "That about covers it for this evening. Let's close in prayer."

If, however, the group is still resolving the tension between ideas when closing time arrives, it is best to recap what conclusion(s) you have reached so far. You can say, "This has been profitable. I think we've made some progress. We've seen that.... Yet, we still need to resolve a couple of issues. So, we'll pick up here when we get back together next week."

If there are some business items which you would like people to remember, such as a social function or a change of meeting location for the next week, mention them at this time. However, avoid returning to a discussion of business items unless the group members strongly feel they would like to do so.

Be sure to end on time. Allow people, however, to stay and enjoy each other's company if they wish (many group leaders will even "reopen" the snack and soft drink table after the group). This way, those who need to leave can do so without requiring everyone to discontinue their conversations, some of which can be more enriching than the group discussion itself.

SUGGESTED FORMAT
FOR THE FIRST MEETING

Objectives

What do you want them to know?
  • the purpose, format, and content of the group
What do you want them to feel?
  • upbeat, safe, accepted, optimistic
What do you want them to do?
  • make the group a part of their schedule, prepare for next week

❏ Mixing

Set out a light snack and drinks; have some soft music playing in the background; create a warm and inviting atmosphere.

❏ Opening

• *Welcome* After you gather everyone together say, **"I'd like to welcome you all here this evening. I'm looking forward to getting to know you, and I hope and pray that you will benefit from our times together. Even though some of us know one another, why don't we begin by going around the room and introducing ourselves?"** At this point you are covering the basic question, *Who are these people?*

• *Purpose and ground rules* Clarify the group's expectations by stating the purpose of the group and discussing ground rules. You are answering the unasked question, *Why am I here?*

One way you can proceed is by saying the following:

"I know I've talked with each of you a little bit about the direction this group will take. We're here to . . . . " (write out in one simple sentence the purpose of the group)

"As we pursue this purpose, I think it will be helpful if we discuss a few simple ground rules and expectations we will have of one another.

"For example, a couple of ground rules I'd like to suggest are, first, that we not repeat outside of the group the things we hear in the group. Maintain confidentiality by letting people tell their own stories" (see pages 46-48 on confidentiality).

"Second, that we allow others the chance to express what they think and feel, but that we do not force one another to talk if they do not wish to.

"What other ground rules do you think we ought to follow?" (The group members may be reluctant to contribute. So you may need to construct the list yourself [see page 24 for a suggested list] Conclude with, "Good. I think this gives us a starting place. We'll return to this list from time to time and add to or modify it as needed."

❏ **Sharing**

After the basic introductions, introduce yourself by sharing your background and interest in the group. Continue with the sharing by saying something like, "I'd like us to get to know one another a little bit better. I'd like to go around the room again and have everyone tell us also where you're from and what kind of work you do."

❏ **Prayer**

Lead the group in a brief prayer; focus on thanks to God for His character and His concerns for us.

❏ **Discussion** (Raise interest in the group by leading a brief discussion on the reasons why the topic will benefit the members; do not try to cover the first lesson.)

• **Hook** (What launching question will you use?)

- **Exploration** (What central issue will be covered in the group over the next several weeks?)

- **Application** (List possible cognitive, affective, and behavioral applications.)
  - Survey the ground rules, format, and content for the group; encourage and answer questions from the group.
  - Be sure everyone has materials.

❑ **Closing**
  - Review any business items members need to remember.

GROUP GROUND RULES

- We encourage you to share as little or as much of your experience as you wish.
- Allow others the chance to express what they think and feel. However, do not force others to talk if they do not wish to.
- We all deal with life in different ways. Avoid passing judgment on others and give advice only with permission.
- Do not repeat outside of the group the things you hear within the group. Maintain confidentiality by letting people tell their own stories. The only exception is when someone's safety or property is in danger.
- Give a good effort to prepare the lessons for each week.
- Pray for and welcome new members.
- Enjoy the relationships you develop here.

WEEKLY SMALL GROUP CHECKLIST

Six days before the group meets
- Prepare the flow of the meeting and discussion
- Collect any special materials needed for the group
- Pray for the group members

Three days before the group meets
- Confirm the location
- Call anyone who missed last week
- Prepare any snacks

Day of the meeting
- Set up signs for directions, if needed
- Set up the chairs in the room
- Set out the snacks
- Check the temperature and lighting
- Turn on the music
- Pray with your co-leaders, if any

MEETING FORMAT WORKSHEET

Objectives

What do you want them to know?

What do you want them to feel?

What do you want them to do?

❑ Mixing

❑ Opening

(Photocopy these pages for your planning each week.)

❑ Sharing (What will you ask them to share about?)

❑ Prayer (If so, who and how long?)

❑ Discussion

  • Hook (What launching question will you use?)

  • Exploration (Which ideas will be held in tension during the group?)

  • Application (List possible cognitive, affective, and behavioral applications.)

❑ **Closing**

Asking Good Questions

Your group discussions live or die based upon the questions you ask. Any question you ask will be leading, closed, or open. A *leading question* ("You agree that God loves you, don't you?") is rhetorical, not discussion-generating. It expects the person to agree. Trial attorneys use this kind of question to force the person giving testimony into a direction in which the attorney wishes to go. The answer is strongly implied in its asking. It may be effective when used appropriately; nevertheless, use it infrequently.

The *limiting question* takes the form of a guessing game. Kids sometimes play the game "Stick Quiz." One child says to another, "I'm thinking of a number between one and ten. What is it?" If the second child guesses wrong, he gets slapped on the back of the hand with a stick or ruler.

You can play the same game with your group by asking questions like, "What two ways can we accomplish this task?" or "What is the main emotion the author expresses here?" If the members guess wrong, you send the non-verbal message, *Wrong! Boy, are you out of it.* People keep guessing until they hit upon the answer you have in mind or, more than likely, they'll quit trying to answer. "Stick Quiz" is a discussion killer. Avoid playing the game while you are leading others to discover the truth.

Limiting questions sometimes resemble exams more than a guessing game. The leader asks a question which tests the knowledge of the participants. For example, while discussing anger in a grief support group a leader may ask, "What three things did Jesus say to His disciples about anger?" Group members are expected to fill in the blank with the correct answer. Grade schoolers sometimes enjoy succeeding at fill-in-the-blank, but adolescents and adults do not like to participate in group discussions when these types of questions are used.

However, for all their weaknesses, limiting questions and, to a lesser degree, leading questions, can play a useful role in a group discussion. For example, by using limiting questions you can help people discover the content of a passage of Scripture. As you teach Titus 2:3-9, for example, you can say, "Notice that in verses four, eight, and ten, Paul includes the clause 'so that...' at the end of each verse. What concern does he reflect in these clauses?" This limiting question causes the group to reflect and synthesize an answer. Notice, however, you should follow this limiting question with an open question such as, "What are some examples of what can happen if we do not reflect a similar concern in our conduct?"

The best way to stimulate discussion is to ask *open questions*. They focus upon who, what, when, where, how, and why; but the answers are not limited to a specific set of data. For example, "Why do you think Paul said, 'Flee immorality' to his readers?" is an open question. With an open question, people's input is valued and their minds are engaged in thinking about the issue at hand. They are not guessing at what answer you are looking for. You communicate that you value their input.

Open questions are frequently begun with phrases like, "In what ways..." "Why do you think..." "How does one..." and "Who do you suppose...." Even the person with little biblical knowledge can become the expert when you ask, "In your opinion...?"

Often group members will ask you to give the correct answer to questions they have. If you answer them directly, you will rob them of the joy of discovering the answer for themselves. You can handle the situation by asking them the question, "What would you say?" or "What do you think?" (these are return questions). Or you can allow others to give their input by asking, "What do the rest of you think?" (here, you are using a relay question).

Setting the Stage

Part of your role as a leader is to set the stage for God to work in people's lives. Attention given to the seemingly unexciting details of a group meeting will provide a better environment in which God can work.

Meeting Site
Select a site for your meeting that is comfortable and accessible. If your small group functions as part of a larger group format (for

example, Sunday School program, women's ministry program, or men's prayer breakfast), the meeting place for your group may already be determined. In this case, you may have little control over the comfort of the room.

On the other hand, you may have more freedom to select the site for your group. A home environment can be a good choice. Many people enjoy the comforts of a living room environment for their church-sponsored small groups. If you meet in your home or the home of a group member, keep in mind the following:

- keep distractions to a minimum; children should be reliably in bed or with a sitter, pets should be restricted, phone calls should be answered by a machine, and the front door should be answered quietly;

- provide comfortable seating; couches and chairs should be arranged so that everyone can see the others in the group, avoid over-crowding;

- minimize entertaining; fancy refreshments, decorations, or dress tend to put people on their social best, they are not free to be themselves during the group interaction; some may perceive the host as wanting to "show off" his or her home and become resentful; and

- make an appropriate room selection; the living room or den is usually best; some climates may allow comfortable use of the patio, but distractions are greater outdoors (wildlife, plane overflights, insects, etc.); do not use a pool-side patio.

Seating Arrangement

Arrange the seating so that each person can see every other person in the group. A circle works best. In addition, place your chair so that it is on the same level as the rest of the group—neither at the focal point of the group nor in the background.

Be aware that the further apart people sit, the less likely they will be to share their thoughts and feelings. Large rooms may be excellent for large groups, but they are killers of discussion unless the seating is placed close together. For example, circle the chairs together in a large classroom, and move the furniture in a living room. This may take a little extra work, but the benefits will be great.

Child Care

If your group members have small children, be sensitive to their ability to obtain reasonably priced child care as you select your group time and location. Some churches encourage the growth of small groups by providing inexpensive or free child care one night a week. Members simply leave their children at the church and proceed to the location of their small group. Other situations will require members to obtain their own child care. In these cases, you might help by gathering a list of reliable and reasonably priced sitters for your group.

Outside Contact

Contact everyone, by phone or in person, for the first two or three weeks your group meets to remind them of the meeting. Once the group has met consistently for three or so weeks, you can assume everyone has it on their calendars and do not need a reminder.

Encourage members of the group to contact anyone who misses the meetings. If you contact them, they may think, *Yeah, you're supposed to call me; you want your group to succeed.* But if, out of genuine concern, another member contacts the person who missed, the person will likely think, *You know, these people care about me.*

In addition, establish a rapport with each group member or married couple outside the small group meeting. This strengthens your relationships with the members by building trust and demonstrating that you care about them. Finally, encourage members to get to know one another through holiday parties and other social events. This provides a way for members to develop deep relationships.

In summary, encourage responsible, healthy relationships outside the group meetings. Be aware, however, that cliques or sexual affairs may occur. They will ultimately devastate the individuals and their families, as well as the group. It may be very helpful to group members for you to lead a discussion on the possibilities and liabilities of an absorbing and exclusive relationship.

Homework

To get the most out of your small groups, the issues discussed during the meeting should also be dealt with outside the meeting. Homework is a good way to help a group member keep working on group issues. Most Rapha books have either a workbook for that purpose or a small group leader's guide with suggested questions which will help group members focus on central concerns.

Be sure everyone has access to the materials with which they are to complete their homework. If people cannot afford the materials, either photo copy materials each week, or provide materials free or on a loan basis.

Non-verbal Communication

Communicate love, acceptance, and warmth non-verbally. For example, if you rarely smile, people will think (often subconsciously) that you do not appreciate them. Additionally, if you have a habit of furrowing your brow when you listen to someone's question, cease and desist. You may actually be thinking about what someone is saying, but it signals displeasure to many people. Likewise, avoid crossing your arms when listening to people. It can communicate a defensive or resistant attitude.

You can also communicate love by appropriate touch. Shake everyone's hand; this is appropriate for both men and women. Be sensitive, however, to people who simply do not want to be touched other than a handshake. You will only increase their feelings of resentment if you attempt to force them to accept touch. Be sure to follow commonly accepted social norms for touch.

Ground Rules

Every group establishes norms consisting of appropriate behaviors for members. This process often occurs subconsciously without discussion. However, your group will benefit if you discuss any group goals, formatting, and expectations at the first meeting and review them from time to time. Most people are not mind-readers and are forgetful as well. In addition, this allows the group to participate in the formulation of the group's ground rules. This takes the spotlight off of you as an autocratic leader and gives the members a sense of ownership in the group (see page 21 on a suggested format for the first meeting).

The Size of Your Group

Discussions are best conducted in groups of about eight to ten people. In groups larger than twelve participants, people do not have enough time to talk and involve themselves in the discussion. On the other hand, group sizes of five people or less can produce low quality discussions.

When inviting people to join your group, keep in mind your ideal group size. If six couples, for example, say they will come to your group, usually you will have six to ten people attend your group each week. However, if you receive commitments from four couples to participate in the group, you may have weeks where only four people show up and your discussion may suffer as a result.

Your group may prosper and swell to over 12 people in size. You can provide people with a greater chance to participate in the discussion by breaking the larger group into two sub-groups during portions of your discussion. Give each of the smaller groups the same question or issue to discuss. After ten to twenty minutes, pull the sub-groups back into one larger group and ask people to share what they learned in the smaller groups. If attendance continues to remain large, consider recruiting another leader and offering two separate groups.

Open Verses Closed Groups

Closed groups limit membership once the group has started. This allows trust to build and relationships to develop without constantly "backtracking" when new members join the group. The weakness is that the group can become inwardly focused and even cliquish. This tends to limit the amount of church growth which can take place through groups.

Alternately, many groups are open to new members at any time during the course of the group. This allows the group to grow. In addition, the numbers of groups will multiply if groups separate into smaller groups when they become too large. Open groups tend to experience less emotional openness and intensity than do the closed groups. Yet, they do not become as engrossed in personal problems and difficulties.

Therapy groups tend to function better as closed groups due to the nature of intense counseling situations. Church growth and support groups benefit by selecting the open group option due to the nature of the church as a growth-by-assimilation body. Your church small group coordinator or pastoral staff will likely want to decide whether your group is opened or closed. If, however, the decision is yours to make, select the open group. You will avoid getting into emotional situations which you are not trained to handle and you will generally enjoy the fresh faces that show up from week to week.

In some cases, you may wish to close your group even if it began as an open group. For example, one woman led a group for three months. During the fourth month, the members began being honest with one another. Then a new member began attending who disrupted the open and safe atmosphere with her domineering behavior. When the new member was present, the older members were silent, but in her absence, they talked freely of their struggles. The leader met with the new member and gently directed her to another group, saying, "We appreciate your coming to our group. But I feel that so-and-so's group might be better suited for you." If you face such a situation and must close your group, help the new member understand that the issue is one of familiarity and stages of personal growth, not one of rejection or acceptance (also see pages 62 and 176 on avoiding an ingrown group).

Recruit a co-leader

As a facilitator of a support group or a leader of a growth group, you may experience powerful and reactionary emotions during the course of the group. You cannot avoid them; it only means you are human.

This reality argues strongly for seeking someone to help you lead the group. Co-leading helps in two ways. First, a co-leader can detect when you get drawn into the emotion of a meeting and lose your effectiveness. For example, a group member may inadvertently criticize your chosen occupation and the character of those who pursue it. You may be hurt and become angry. You may even become vulnerable to the temptation to take revenge in some subtle form (such as through humor). A trusted co-leader can give you feedback concerning your reactions to the group members and your overall effectiveness as a leader. Part of this feedback process involves your ability to "blow off steam" (as it were) with a trusted co-leader concerning the people or situations you face.

Second, a co-leader can assist you in the running of the group. He or she can substitute for you should you become ill, help manage the details of the group business, or handle portions of the group meeting itself. Having someone to share the burdens of the group helps increase your ability to lead groups for more than a season.

The major guidelines for selecting a co-leader or co-facilitator are a mutual respect and an open line of communication. It is doubtful, and even undesirable, that the co-leaders agree on everything said and done in the group. Differences in personality, approach, and experience add to the richness of co-leading. Yet, unless the leaders respect one another, these differences will erupt into conflict and will negatively influence the effectiveness of the group. Likewise, unless time is allotted for talking together about the direction of the group, even when the leaders respect one another, confusion, frustration, and misdirection can occur in the group meetings.

Managing Difficulties

Whenever you gather a group of people together you will encounter difficulties. Some of them are minor and easily managed. Some, however, require a bit more training and input.

The Excessive Talker

Sometimes you will have a member of your group who will dominate the group discussion. They may talk excessively about themselves, tell detailed stories, or even redirect the group discussion in a different direction than the one you planned. In effect, they will control the tenor and agenda of the group.

Excessive talkers will drain the life of a group. First, they simply do not allow others to contribute while they are talking. Second, group members will come to resent his or her comments and behaviors. Finally, excessive talkers tend to steer the group discussion away from feelings and in-depth responses toward a more superficial level of interaction.

As the leader, you need to deal with the situation created by the excessive talker. You can accomplish this by being subtle at first. Later you may need to be more direct. Always keep in mind that excessive talkers are not problems that need to be settled, but people who have problems which need resolution.

First, look for breaks in the person's comments, either in his ideas or simply when he takes a breath. Quickly ask the group, "What do the rest of you think?" After some group response, move onto another issue or point in the discussion. If this fails to involve others in the discussion, try saying, "I know what you're getting at, but let's hear what some others have to say."

Finally, you may have to speak to the person after the group meeting and say something like, "I appreciate your comments and I'm glad you feel free to participate in the discussion. However, you need to limit your comments so others can contribute as well." The person may experience hurt feelings, so be as gentle as you are firm.

As your group leading skills improve and the group matures, you can help excessive talkers by raising in the group the issues they create. The goal is not to put them in their place, but to help them to understand why they talk so much and to gain insight into how their talkativeness affects others. Excessive talkers are often unaware of how their conversational style is perceived by others. Dealing with the issue in the group can help excessive talkers grow.

You may say something like, "Terry, I cannot help but notice that you contribute much more than the others to the group discussion.

Why do you think that's so?" After the person's response, you can say to the group, "How do the rest of you perceive Terry's role in our discussions?"

Again, this should only be done in a mature group where trust has been established. Where trust is undeveloped, not only will talkative people not be receptive to any observations, but other group members will become very cautious in their group involvement. When in doubt, leave this approach out.

The Silent Person

Compared to the excessive talker, the silent person may seem like a blessing to some leaders. Yet, silent people also have needs which can be met in the group. Silent people may be resistant or shy. They may feel like they have nothing worthwhile to say. They may fear looking foolish or being rejected. Whatever the case, they use silence as a means of withdrawing from the group.

Do not pressure them into contributing or criticize them for their silence. Instead, encourage their participation by listening to, appreciating, and affirming their comments. You may wish to approach them privately and let them know that many people misinterpret silence. Ask them what their silence means and how you can encourage their participation.

Conflicts

As people begin discussing their lives and responses in the group, you may notice them saying things like, "You shouldn't feel that way," "You frustrate me," or "You don't care!" In a manner of speaking, this can be a positive sign—members are becoming more free in their communication. Yet, you need to direct this freedom by encouraging people to take responsibility for their own emotions. You can do this by encouraging members to talk in terms of "I" and not "you."

For example, "I feel bad when you say...to me" is preferred to "YOU make me angry when you say...to me." Other examples include, "I get frustrated when you...," "I don't perceive that you care" or "I feel hurt (or angry)...."

This approach will not eliminate conflict, but it will contribute greatly to your ability to manage the conflict so that it does not rupture the group. In addition, group members will learn an effective and constructive skill in dealing with conflicts they may face outside the group (see pages 60-61 for more on dealing with conflict).

Language

From time to time you may find members of your group using coarse or profane language, especially when they become emotionally involved in what they are saying. You may be tempted to quote Ephesians 4:29, "Do not let any unwholesome talk come out of your mouths, but only what is helpful for building others up...." While we all should heed Paul's command, the way we implement God's Word in this kind of situation can help or hinder people's ability to express themselves.

Acknowledge members' emotions that gave rise to profanity. Then suggest other ways of expressing themselves. You can begin, for example, by saying, "You seem really angry, Lee. What are you most angry about?" After Lee has explained his anger, you can then suggest another way of expressing that anger in more appropriate words. You might say, "I can understand why you are angry. But I think others might be offended at the way you expressed it." Then turn to the group and ask, "How would you suggest Lee express his anger?" When approached in this manner, you will be more likely to encourage the application of Ephesians 4:29 than if you communicate, "Read and heed!"

Inappropriate topics

Invariably someone in the group will bring up a subject which should not be discussed in a group. For example, they may reveal confidential information or describe private matters such as sexual behaviors. Although it may have already been decided that certain subjects are off limits, the group leader may expect this to happen at least once and should be prepared to deal with the problem. For example, you can say, "I can understand your desire to talk about this. However, this might not be a good time. Others in the group might feel uncomfortable and we may be breaching confidentiality.

I'd like to talk about this with you later, if you wish. But we need to move on."

Feedback

An important benefit of a small group is the opportunity to see yourself through another person's eyes. As a group member expresses his thoughts and feelings, others in the group gain impressions about the one speaking based upon what is said as well as how it is presented. When honest feedback is offered in response, the one sharing is able to find out how other people see him. The results are sometimes quite surprising and usually helpful to everyone in the group.

Often, however, people in the group volunteer this feedback in a destructive way. Instruct the group that feedback should only be given when requested. For example, Sally may be telling everyone how much she resents her ex-husband. Janet desires to contribute her own observations and should ask, "May I give you feedback on what you're saying?" Only if Sally agrees is Janet free to say something like, "I perceive that you are not willing to forgive your ex-husband for causing you so much trouble. Is that the case?"

Advice Giving

The very purpose of a growth or support group is to provide people with solutions for life. This should be even more true for a biblically based group. Yet, solutions suggested too quickly through the giving of advice can hamper effective problem solving in at least three ways.

First, those who experience difficulties in life need to come to terms with their losses. Major difficulties and, to a lesser extent, compounding minor hassles either result from or contribute to the death of dreams and hopes. Dealing with these losses takes time. Quick advice often attempts to short-circuit this process.

Second, it is better to learn how to solve problems than to have someone give you the answer. Advice givers, in effect, attempt to solve others' problems. Their advice may be sound, but the way they give it does not help people learn how to construct solutions for themselves. The familiar maxim is quite applicable, "If I give you a fish, you will eat for a day; if I teach you to fish, you will eat for a lifetime."

Third, quick advice is often superficial. While it appears to answer the problems, in reality, it does not deal with the significant issues. Biblical answers are profound, but they can be used in a simplistic way when wisdom is absent.

If people in your group are prone to offering advice, have them discuss the implications of the following proverbs for the group.

> *Like one who takes away a garment on a cold day, or like vinegar poured on soda, is one who sings songs to a heavy heart.*
>
> Proverbs 25:20

> *He who answers before listening—that is his folly and his shame.*
>
> Proverbs 18:13

> *Reckless words pierce like a sword, but the tongue of the wise brings healing.*
>
> Proverbs 12:18

> *A simple man believes anything, but a prudent man gives thought to his steps.*
>
> Proverbs 14:15

Some implications you can suggest to the group include:
- offer advice only when you have taken time to understand, mentally and emotionally, the person's condition;
- offer advice only when you have taken time to consider the implications of your advice; and
- do not offer advice in an effort to get people to "cheer up."

When to Refer

As a support group leader or facilitator, you may notice group members having difficulty functioning in their daily lives. They may, for example, be experiencing stress. We all experience major stress from time to time including changes in employment, promotions at work, moves to new residences, marriage, birth of children, sickness or death of family members or close friends, reversal of financial status, and debt. Sometimes these stressors occur at the same time.

Whenever stressful events occur, our normal ways of coping with life are placed under strain. Our ability to function in daily life may begin to falter. Often, problems we have had in the past, such as depression, anxiety, or various addictions, may resurface. Or, current problems may simply get worse. Group members may need help which lies beyond your ability to assist.

In such cases, you should seriously consider suggesting to that person that he get professional help. The table on the following page outlines the major areas in which people often experience difficulty.

MOOD
Depressed facial expression
Extreme anxiety
Excessive enthusiasm
Sleep disturbance
Suicidal thoughts
Social withdrawal

THOUGHT
Hallucinations
Confusion
Judgement impaired
Delusions
Memory loss
Phobias/panic attacks

VIOLENCE
Homicidal thoughts
Aggressive behavior
Child/sexual abuse

COMPULSIVE/SUBSTANCE ABUSE
Binge/purge/starve with food
Alcohol/drug abuse
Sexual acting out

CHANGE IN VOCATIONAL or EDUCATIONAL FUNCTION
Change in school/job function
Marital/family/child conflict

BEHAVIOR DISORDERS
Running away
Fire setting

Most people are unqualified to decide whether someone has a significant problem in any of these areas. Contact your pastor for help. Also, Rapha Hospital Treatment Centers offers free assessment and referral, 24 hours a day. To contact a Rapha assessment counselor call 1-800-383-HOPE (see page 127 for more on when to refer).

Evaluation Questions

1. Indicate whether the following questions are leading, limiting, or open.

   • What does God say about anger?

   • How often did Jesus say we should forgive people who have harmed us?

   • Don't you think we should "get it off our chest" when we're angry?

   • What does I Corinthians 13:10 say? Who can quote that?

   • How do you feel when Jesus says, "You cannot serve God and money"?

   Rephrase the leading and limiting questions above and make them open questions.

2. How would you explain the difference between a group which uses open questions and one that allows any answer, biblical or not, to stand unchallenged?

3. Which of the following potential difficulties are the hardest for you to manage? What do you need to do in order to improve (e.g., increase skills, gain experience, or overcome a fear of failure, a desire to be liked, or a need to rescue people from their problems)?

   ❏　the excessive talker
   ❏　the silent person
   ❏　conflicts
   ❏　inappropriate language and topics
   ❏　feedback
   ❏　advice giving
   ❏　knowing when to refer

3

THE DYNAMICS OF A GROUP

Objectives:

- to give an understanding of the elements of an effective small group;
- to provide an overview of the stages of a small group; and
- to give insights into what motivates people to join or lead a small group.

In the previous chapter, we focused on what you should do to get a small group up and running. In this chapter, we give you some of the reasoning behind those practical suggestions. Knowing the reasons why some groups progress while others do poorly will help you gain more control over the course of your group. You will be able to detect potential problems and understand what will be needed in order to enhance the effectiveness of your group.

Group dynamics refers to the life and growth of the group and of the individuals who attend. The stages of interaction between members over time are affected by the group environment and the character and skills of the group leader. The following material is drawn from a combined experience of over forty years in leading small groups. Even so, we also draw upon the insights of others, especially Corey and Corey (*Groups: Process and Practice*, 3d ed., Pacific Grove, CA: Brooks/Cole, 1987).

Elements of an Effective Small Group Environment

Several key elements contribute significantly to an environment in which God can change lives. Any of these elements alone can stimulate growth in people. Each element, however, contributes to the effectiveness of the other elements. Thus, the combination of these elements in your group is a powerful tool in God's hands.

Love and acceptance

As the leader, if you regularly display love and acceptance in the group, you will provide a safe environment for change. People need to know that others care for them. On the positive side, you display that love by accepting people regardless of where they are in their spiritual life. By showing interest in people, listening to their ideas and concerns, appreciating their contribution and affirming their value, you can show others that you accept them.

On the negative side, if you frequently correct people's ideas, ridicule the opinions of others who are not members of the group, frown a lot, make sarcastic jokes, or even wait for others to initiate conversations with you, you communicate a lack of acceptance. You may genuinely love people, but unless you communicate that love verbally and non-verbally, others may not perceive your love. To accept someone does not mean you approve of everything that person does. For example, God accepts His children because of what Christ has done. Yet, He does not approve of all that His children choose to do. He loves and accepts us as His children even though we still sin.

Safety and trust

Provide a safe place. Significant change in patterns of living and thinking is risky. People need a safe place in which to think about the changes God wants them to make in their lives. They need to feel secure in order to consider serious changes in long-term patterns of relating to God and others. Therefore, you need to develop an atmosphere of trust and stability. Your loving and accepting people without precondition contributes significantly to their personal security. If people know they will not be rejected for what they say or do, they will feel safe in your acceptance. Yet, you can further build a secure atmosphere in your group through maintaining confidentiality and consistency.

Confidentiality. After a measure of trust has developed in an atmosphere of unconditional love, members will begin to reveal sensitive facets of their lives to the group. If a member shares this information with someone who is not a member of the group, confidentiality is then broken and mutual trust may be seriously handicapped.

Sometimes members of the group will ask you, as the leader, for advice on private matters. If you later mention what you know of their situation to the group, you will have signalled to the rest of the group your inability to keep information in confidence. You may also have seriously eroded the trust these people placed in you when they sought your advice.

Perhaps the most common way in which confidentiality is breached in Christian circles is through the sharing of prayer requests. What begins as well-intentioned concern often turns into a non-vicious form of gossip which is, nonetheless, hurtful. This often occurs when people wish to "pray specifically" for a person's needs and they inquire about the details of the situation. As they share this "prayer concern" to others, they convert private matters into public knowledge. Confidentiality is lost and the safe environment of the group is compromised. A simple rule for maintaining confidence is, "Let people tell their own stories," or said another way, "Tell your own story, not someone else's." By following this maxim, you will avoid betraying others' confidence.

The only exception to this position on confidentiality is when someone volunteers information that reveals a danger, actual or threatened, to someone's safety or property. In most states, people who are aware of these threats must report them to the proper authorities. For example, if someone reveals a situation where child abuse is occurring, the group leader, and other members as well, must report this knowledge to the state's Child Protective Services. Or, if a man says, "I'm so mad at my company for firing me, I'm going to burn it down. And I know just how to do it, too," you must report this threat to the police. Someone may even mention his desire to end his own life. This, too, is an exception to the principle of confidentiality.

In light of these possibilities, you may wish to mention this exception in your first group meeting. For example, you can read the statement of confidentiality and then add, "The only exceptions are any mention of a danger to someone's safety or property. In these cases, everyone in the group is bound by law to report these situations to the proper authorities."

Consistency. People, on the whole, unconsciously look for patterns of reliability before they place their trust in others. Your consistency will contribute to group members' ability to trust both you and the rest of the group.

Consistency is reflected in a variety of tangible ways. For example, starting and ending your group on time, meeting at the same place and time each week, and following the same meeting format communicate consistency. Less tangible actions also affect the overall impression of consistency. The group leader who is sporadically available for conversation outside the group or who displays periodic rejection of other's opinions will experience difficulty establishing an atmosphere of consistency. Absolute consistency is not possible or, perhaps, even desirable. Yet, you can strive for an overall pattern of reliability in what you say and do.

Empathy and comfort

Most people want to be understood, especially if they are going through difficult times. Even when life's circumstances are fairly stable, knowing that someone else understands gives comfort. When you lend an empathetic ear you display a deep understanding of their situation. You are, in effect, saying, *You are not alone.* And that comforts people. The Apostle Paul instructed the early church to "rejoice with those who rejoice, weep with those who weep," and speaks of God as the "God of all comfort" and the One "who comforts the downcast" (Romans 12:14; II Corinthians 1:3; 7:6). By modeling God's comforting character in your group, you provide God the opportunity to change lives.

Active listening plays a central role in empathy. We often listen to others while thinking about how we are going to respond. An active listener, on the other hand, is not primarily concerned with his own response. Rather, he focuses not only upon what a person is saying but upon the thoughts and feelings revealed by the speaker. This focus allows the listener to feel, in a limited way, the feelings of the speaker.

Hope and encouragement

Comfort in the present leads to hope for the future and the encouragement we all need to go on. If people have reason to hope and their hopes are realistic, they can endure the process of change. The balance between admitting the scope of one's problems and developing a hope for change can be a delicate one. For example, you may notice the members of your group becoming gloomy and depressed as they realize the difficulties they face. You will need to encourage them without minimizing the difficult task before them.

Power and control

Many people have been victimized during their lives. The abuse may have been emotional, physical, or sexual, and may have occurred in childhood and adulthood alike. Yet, individuals need to see themselves as more than victims. They need a sense of power and control over their own lives. Your group can help people grasp the fact that they do have choices, that they have the ability to gain control over the way they live.

To many Christians this sounds like a concession to self-centeredness. Yet, the need for a sense of power and control over our lives does not necessarily run counter to a Christ-centered life. God enables us to make responsible choices. We can either choose to follow His leadership and trust in His resources in our lives, or we can choose to follow our own inclinations and trust in our own abilities. The ability to make that choice is based in a sense of personal power and control in our lives. We should willingly choose to submit to His direction and power, not as victims but as volunteers.

God provides people the power they need to change. For example, Paul wrote Timothy, "For God has not given us a spirit of timidity, but a spirit of power, of love, and of self-discipline" (II Timothy 1:7). Elsewhere, he prays for his readers that God "may strengthen you with power through his Spirit in your inner being" (Ephesians 3:16). God wishes through His Spirit and His power to strengthen and empower us at the core of who we are. God does not oppose personal power and control. He opposes misused personal power and control, a personal power and control used in rebellion against Him. Your group can encourage people, "You have the power and ability to change."

Openness and honesty

People are more likely to change when they perceive the need to do so. Yet, people are often reluctant to acknowledge their needs. By fostering open and honest group interaction, you model for people the honesty required to admit a need to change.

We can be honest in a couple of ways. First, we can be honest with ourselves about ourselves; this requires vulnerability. If you, for example, can admit to yourself that you are at times fearful, you have made the first step toward changing your fear. If, in addition, you can admit your fear to the group, you are telling the group, *It's okay to admit your fears.*

Second, we can be honest with others about how we perceive or feel about them; this requires love. "Brutal honesty," however, should not be allowed. Paul instructed his readers to "...put off falsehood and speak truthfully to his neighbor, for we are all members of one body" (Ephesians 4:25). He also said to speak "the truth in love" (Ephesians 4:15). When a person is honest about how he or she feels about or perceives another, he or she should focus upon the well-being of others.

Freedom of expression

Give people the freedom to express their thoughts and feelings, hopes and dreams, and fears and failures. Not everyone will share these things with the group to the same degree or depth, especially in the early stages of your group. Yet, you should provide the freedom for them to do so if they wish. Allow opportunities for people to talk, feel, and act during the group as you plan for each session. Give people the opportunity to sample new ideas, perspectives, and feelings. This includes the use of open-ended and feeling-oriented questions, a relaxed atmosphere, a non-judgmental attitude, and even silence.

When people experience love and acceptance, they will often express how they really feel about the situations in their lives. They may even express pent-up feelings in powerful ways by bursting into sobs, shaking uncontrollably, or speaking quite harshly about others who have harmed them. This emotional release can be a healthy way for people to face the truth about how they really feel. Yet, emotional release, by itself, carries with it little long-term benefit. People need to be able to place their emotions into perspective in order to deal effectively with them.

Information and Perspective

People need to know what to think and do when they encounter new difficulties in life. Even in the absence of stress, people want and need to learn how to grow in their walk with God and in their relationships with family, friends, and co-workers. Remember to include factual information in your weekly meetings about the topic that has brought the group members together. Discussion which focuses on causes, symptoms, and remedies for the difficulties and challenges of life is a necessary part of any successful small group.

As mentioned above, emotional release alone is not sufficient to produce long-term benefits and changes. People need to couple this release with a new perspective, a new way of looking at things, so they can interpret their emotions and responses to hurtful situations. The information you provide (not by a lecture, but through a discussion format) can assist the group members in putting their emotional experience into words. In this way, they can gain the perspective they need in order to make responsible changes in their responses to people.

Each of these elements may not be present in your group each time it meets. For example, you may spend most of your time one week comforting people who have encountered difficult situations. As a result, you will be high in comfort and low in information (because you ran out of time). You can, however, strive for an overall balance between the elements.

In addition, you will find that you will have strengths which cause you to emphasize a certain element or two. For example, your group's strengths may be freedom of expression and honesty and, yet, the content may be lacking. Be grateful for your strengths and devote a little extra effort to improving the other areas.

Dynamics of Group Leadership

You could probably fill yards of shelf space with recent books which discuss the essential characteristics and skills of leadership in general and group leadership in particular. Our discussion will not replace these books, but will focus upon the essential elements you will need for leading your small group.

The character of the leader

The essential element in the effectiveness of your group is you. Your content, skills, techniques, preparation, and ideas are all important. Yet, who you are, not just what you do, is the common denominator. Time spent on development of your character will yield the most benefit for your group. In his recent book, *How to Get Along with Almost Anyone*, H. Norman Wright notes the three basic qualities needed to get along well with a variety of people. These same qualities, genuineness, nonpossessive love, and empathy, also play a key role in your effectiveness as a group leader.

Genuineness. To be an effective group leader or facilitator you must be genuine. The apostle Paul insisted that church leaders possess this quality and displayed it in his dealings with the churches (I

Timothy 3:8; 2 Corinthians 1:12). Genuine people encourage trust, and people feel safe with a genuine group leader. Synonyms of "genuine" are authentic, bona fide, original, valid, veritable, guileless, natural, sincere, unaffected, and unfeigned. When you are genuine no one has to read between the lines, no one has to interpret you, no one has to wonder if you are really what you say you are. Genuine people do not wear masks or put on fronts. They are real.

Transparency and openness are related to genuineness. Being open and transparent does not mean you "spill your guts" to everyone you meet. Something is wrong with the person who shares his most personal failures with a cab driver. Transparency means being seen for who you really are, not by everyone, but to those with whom you share a personal relationship. It involves honesty and integrity; what you are in public (in the eyes of others) is what you are in private.

Nonpossessive love. The second essential quality possessed by an effective group leader is a nonpossessive love. Loving others is second only to loving God and is the mark of authentic Christianity (Matthew 22:37-39; John 13:35, 17:23; I John 4:7-8; 20). Many people confuse love with sentimentality or emotions. However, the biblical authors focus upon the action of love, not its emotions. Sentiment and emotion may accompany love, but its essence is action. For example, Jesus was not sentimental or warmly emotional as He hung on the cross, yet He conclusively displayed God's love. Loving actions include: caring, kindness, gentleness, respect, fairness, and even rebuke, which come from a motivation to build and not destroy the person.

Nonpossessive love distinguishes between the person and the deeds. For example, Jesus displayed nonpossessive love in His encounter with a rich young man. Though He loved the man, He allowed him to walk away from eternal life (Mark 10:17-23). Love does not blur the boundaries between individuals but allows others to express their own individuality, even if their choices are wrong. We can disapprove of and even limit people's misbehavior and still love them.

Empathy. Empathy is defined as the "identification with and understanding of another's situation, feelings, and motives" (*The New American Heritage Dictionary*). It involves seeing another's world through his or her eyes, and gives others the great sense they are understood. Wright distinguishes between empathy, sympathy, and apathy. He observes, "Apathy has no feelings, sympathy is feeling for another; and empathy is feeling with another. Apathy says, *I don't care*; sympathy says, *Oh, you poor thing*; and empathy says, *It looks like you're having a difficult time today.*" People do not want our sympathy, much less our apathy; they want our empathy.

It should be obvious that many thousands of work-related meetings are conducted each day, very few of which are characterized by the above qualities. Task-oriented groups can function without genuineness, nonpossessive love, and empathy. Yet, people will not likely grow in their personal and spiritual lives without these elements being present in their leaders.

The basic skills of the leader

Character deals with who we are; skill with what we do. Successful groups depend to a large degree upon what we do. Those who possess more of the qualities listed above will reap the greatest results from developing their skills. Yet, regardless of our character, we all need to refine our group leading skills.

Active listening. The active listener is one who is alert to all the levels of communication being used by a speaker. When people speak up in a small group (or anywhere else), they use more than words to communicate with others. They use changes in tone of voice, body posture, and word choice to communicate their thoughts and feelings. Active listeners are alert to these signals and the messages they communicate.

Sometimes people send conflicting messages. For example, a man may be talking about the peace of God in his life and yet display considerable agitation through his harsh tone of voice and clinched fists. Or, a young woman may say, "I hate my mother for not shielding me from my father. But she's such a weak person and

I love her." Group leaders need to pay particularly close attention because conflicting messages are often separated by several minutes, sometimes even days or weeks.

You can increase your active listening skills by becoming aware of the factors, both external and internal, which cause you to give too little attention to what other people are saying. External distractions can usually be corrected easily, such as when loud noises occur in the adjoining room or hallway. Internal distractions require more awareness and effort to overcome. For example, you may be upset because you quarreled with your spouse just before leaving home for the group meeting. As a result, you will likely not be able to listen as attentively as you otherwise might. In this situation, the distraction is temporary, unless, of course, you quarrel frequently. Other distractions are more pervasive, such as when a leader fears facing possible rejection if the group falters. Group leaders must work harder to surmount these barriers to active listening.

Encouraging openness. Leaders who learn to draw people out and involve them in the group will increase their group's cohesiveness and, hence, their effectiveness as a leader. Encouraging people to share themselves includes asking people about themselves, what they think, what they feel, what their family is like, and what their interests and hobbies are. It also entails valuing and affirming them and, conversely, avoiding personal attacks and criticisms. By doing this, you communicate, *You matter to me and to this group. You can make a contribution.*

Drawing people out pivots on the attitude of the leader toward the group members. Leaders who view members as "lost sheep" in desperate need of direction will have a difficult time involving people in the group. Group members will likely assume the role of passive receivers of information and control. On the other hand, leaders who hold people in high regard will make ample room for the contributions of group members. Members become actively involved in the group and contribute to others.

Facilitating. The difference between encouraging openness and facilitating is one of focus. Drawing people out focuses on urging individuals to share themselves with others. Facilitating focuses upon the group as a whole once people begin to communicate and contribute. One precedes the other, but both are closely linked. Corey and Corey, in *Groups: Process and Practice*, lists ways leaders can facilitate group interaction. They can: 1) assist members to express honestly their fears and expectations; 2) work to create an atmosphere of safety and acceptance; 3) encourage and support members as they explore new ideas and behaviors; 4) involve as many people as possible in the interaction; 5) work to lessen dependency upon the group leader; 6) encourage open expression of conflict and controversy; and 7) help members remove hindrances to direct communication. In short, cultivate open and responsible communication.

Knowing limits. You will likely face situations which exceed your ability to handle effectively. Indeed, very few professionals can deal with every type of problem people face. You will need to: 1) seek outside advice for yourself as you deal with group situations, or 2) refer a group member to a more qualified resource. By knowing your limits, you can avoid a lot of grief for yourself and for your group members.

For example, someone in your group may say, "I've given this some thought and I'm leaving my wife." Unless you have training and experience in marriage counseling, you should refer this person to your pastor or a Christian marriage and family counselor in your area. Likewise, if someone volunteers, "I don't feel like life is worth living," "I've recently had flashbacks of my father visiting my bedroom late at night," or "I sometimes hear voices and can't find who's speaking," you should suggest that person talk with a Christian professional counselor (see pages 40-42, and 127 on when to refer).

Stages of Development of a Small Group Leader

Group leaders go through stages as they develop in their leadership skills. They may spend anywhere from a few minutes to a few weeks or months in each stage. Training, experience, and feedback from more experienced leaders can help you move through these stages.

Stage One: Focus on Self

Inexperienced leaders usually fear the prospect of failing in their groups. Consequently, they tend to center upon how they will be perceived and focus mostly upon their performance. They may ask questions like, "How am I doing?" or "Do these people like me?" During the group discussion, leaders in this stage will be anxious. They will likely talk too much, speak rapidly, feel uncomfortable with silence, or fail to listen actively to the members' comments (because they are thinking about what they are going to say next). As a result, the members will not feel relaxed and secure, and they will take fewer risks in talking about the real issues of life.

Stage Two: Focus on Content

After leaders feel secure, they will shift their attention to the content of the group discussion. The accuracy, relevancy, and clarity of the content occupy their minds as they thoroughly prepare the "lesson." Questions which dominate their thoughts include, "Is this content any good?" "Is it worthwhile?" "Does it hold people's interest?"

A group led by a person in this content-oriented stage may display the following traits:

- too much reliance upon the group leader as he or she consults tightly worded and constructed notes;
- little room for other ideas in the discussion;
- too much focus upon ideas and too little expression of feelings and emotion;

- group discussion is minimal and the leader shifts to a lecture style of communication to fill the void; and
- focus is centered upon the leader and not upon the relationships and interaction of the group.

Stage Three: Focus on People

Experienced leaders tend to focus upon the welfare of the group members. Areas of concern include: *How is the group interacting together? How is each member responding; how does he or she feel? Are the members growing as individuals and as a group?* The effective small group leader functions at this level on a regular basis.

The "Ideal" Group Leader

This manual includes the insights of seasoned group leaders. We have selected the best advice available from a variety of sources. Yet, no one individual perfectly follows all the advice given or exhibits all the qualities and skills of an effective group leader. Each person possesses unique strengths and abilities which enable him or her to excel in one or two areas of group leadership. Very few people excel in every area. You may be overwhelmed with the thought of leading a group "by the manual." Take courage: God can and will use you if you seek to prepare to the best of your ability, trust Him throughout the process, and love your group members.

As you start your first group, remember, "Love covers a multitude of sins" (I Peter 4:8). Many people stumble through the mechanics of a small group, clueless as to what they are trying to accomplish, yet they experience success because they love the members of the group. Even if you fail in your first few attempts at leading a group, God can use your experience to develop your leadership skills—if you keep going. Most successful leaders can tell stories of their own group failures. The only difference between you and them is the time it takes to learn from one's mistakes.

Stages of a Small Group

Each newly-formed group progresses through various stages as the members identify with one another. Through understanding these stages you can gain insight into the responses you receive from the group. You will also understand how to meet the needs of group members during these stages.

Stage One: Exploration

As most people join a group, they are asking themselves (consciously or unconsciously) the following questions.

Who are these people?
Will I be in or out of this group?
If I join, how involved will I be?
Do I belong here; will they accept me?
Do these people like me; do I like them?
How much do I want to risk?
Can I really trust these people?
What's this group really about?
What's expected of me?
Do I fit and belong in here?
Can I be myself and be a part of this group?

In doing so, they are exploring the group and its possibilities. In this stage, people tend to give only basic information about themselves and accept others on a superficial level. They experience various levels of anxiety and are hesitant and insecure. Periods of awkward silence will occur in the group.

The group leader can best help the group members navigate the first stage by establishing trust through the creation of an atmosphere of security. People need to feel safe, especially if they are expected to talk about themselves in any fashion. You can develop people's sense of security by doing the following.

Display a commitment to the group. By your commitment to preparation, punctuality, consistency, and enthusiasm you communicate that you are "in there" with the group members. Communicate expectations. Cover the ground rules weekly. Adhere to them consistently. Be sure to include the members in the formulation of the ground rules.

Take individual interest in the group members. Give attention to remembering people's names, dealing with their concerns, and appreciating their contributions. This affirms each member's value and creates security.

Deal positively with people's concerns. If you discount a member's concern over, let's say, child care, you signal not only your insensitivity but your lack of commitment to them.

Respond properly to negative emotions. As members feel comfortable in the group, negative and profound emotions may surface. Someone may become angry or cry, for example. If you subtly try to scold them for their anger or display an awkwardness at their tears, you will effectively signal that people should control their emotions in the group. Their trust will be limited to the exchange of ideas and opinions, and your effectiveness as a leader will be limited.

Remember: your group members are depending on you. Your honesty, spontaneity, genuineness, and warmth communicates, *I am a safe person*, and people will trust your leadership.

Stage Two: Transition

Typically, your group will go through a transition from the exploring phase to the working stage. Positive elements of an effective group will begin to emerge. Yet, some members may also display less enthusiasm and more impatience and anxiety. Attendance may suffer. Sometimes this transition period may be marked by a struggle for control of the group. This struggle may be subtle and smoldering and may erupt later into full conflict. During this stage, members will increasingly face such questions as, *How much will I disclose about myself? Is this really a safe place? Will people reject me? What do they think of me so far?* They may also enter into conflicts with one another, label people as "problem cases," or refuse to trust the group. Naturally, the group leader needs to be prepared for a challenge of his leadership.

The best way to handle this conflict is to deal with it openly and honestly. If you ignore, discount, or fight the challenge, you are actually modeling behaviors which contradict the intention of the group—the development of trust which leads to change. For example, you might begin by saying, "I detect some conflict here, what do you all think?" As you discuss the issue, your honesty, lack of defensiveness, and acceptance of people will provide a constructive model for the group. In general, you can help members move through this stage by dealing sensitively with negative feelings. This involves resolving conflicts but also encouraging people as they make progress.

Stage Three: Working

Group members in this stage are thinking, "Let's accomplish something together." They are willing to work as they grow together. Cohesiveness is the distinguishing mark of this stage. Other traits of this stage include the following.

Trust and acceptance. Members trust one another and the leader. Trust is evident by their willingness to take risks in talking about their personal concerns.

Empathy and caring. Members display their care by a deep and subjective understanding of one another's situations.

Hope. Members desire change and believe that it is attainable.

Commitment to change. Members grow when they know what to change and how to go about it. Commitment is evident when individuals follow through with their plans to make things different.

Intimacy. People feel liked and they like one another; they feel close to one another.

Self-disclosure. Members are honest with one another about what they think, feel, and do.

For all the positive elements of this stage, at least three pitfalls exist. First, your group may become a closed group at this point. Everyone may have agreed from the outset to keep the group open to new people. Yet, the group can close itself to outsiders in practice when members develop the attitude, *No one knows and understands me like the people in this group, and other people will only get in the way of deepening our relationships.* If this occurs, bring it to the attention of the group. For example, you could say, "It's my impression that we've drifted from our concern to include new people in the group. What do you all think? What in our attitudes encourages a closed stance? How can we rekindle our desire to minister to new people?"

Secondly, your group may become comfortable with each other to such a degree that individual growth stops. Members quit challenging one another as they lose their intensity to change. As a result, the group can lose its focus and purpose for existence. Your role as a leader is to continue to provide a balance between encouragement and challenge, between comfort and confrontation.

Finally, the group may begin to criticize the church leadership. The potential for this exists in churches whose members have felt lonely and uncared for (for whatever reason). When these people begin to feel loved in your group, some may begin to express attitudes such as, *Why hasn't the church met my needs like this before? I've attended this church for over five years and this is the first time someone has shown me what love is all about.* Some members may begin to "bash the pastor" in the group. Deal with this by, first, recognizing the ego-flattering nature of this criticism (*I've succeeded where all others have failed*) and resist it. Second, challenge the group to consider, "It seems we're bitter or resentful toward the church leadership. What do you all think? What does this say about us?"

Motives for Group Involvement

People become involved in small groups, either as a member or as a leader, for a variety of conscious and unconscious reasons. Members also bring with them a variety of fears and concerns about the group itself. By understanding how these motivations and de-motivations influence people's actions, you can better meet their needs.

Fears people bring to a group

Most of our fears are unvoiced and many are even unconscious. Yet, their presence guides and shapes our responses to people and situations. Often, simply describing a fear does much to neutralize its effects in our lives. For example, many of our relationships are guided by a fear of rejection. We may not be constantly and consciously aware of that fear, yet it prevents us from stepping out and meeting new people. Once we gain an awareness of our fear of rejection, we can then examine it and begin to control our fear instead of allowing our fear to control us.

Fear of being known. Even though people may be lonely, they are fearful of being known. Many people share the secret fear, *If they only knew what I was really like, they would not want to be my friend.* As a consequence, they reveal very little of their true thoughts and feelings. Others fear appearing foolish or ignorant, so they speak up or invite conversation with others only with reluctance. You can help people overcome their fear of being known by affirming their contributions. This involves listening respectfully, preventing arguments, and appreciating their input. In addition, you should deflect away from them pressure to participate in the group. This will allow them the freedom to contribute to the group when they feel comfortable.

Fear of being betrayed. People resent the betrayal of trust that occurs when something said in confidence is passed on to others. When the broken confidence is compounded by a misrepresentation of their lives to others, hurt and anger almost certainly result. The pain of these experiences causes people to fear being betrayed, so they typically reveal only the aspects of their lives which are already generally known. Fear of betrayal can be eased by insisting, "The things said in the group should remain in the group," or "Let people tell their own story." This should be done in word (for example, during the reading of the ground rules) and in deed (for example, asking someone to stop telling another's story).

Fear of disappointment. We have all experienced unfulfilled hopes and dreams. As a result, we insulate ourselves from too much hope. We think, *If I expect bad things to happen, I won't be disappointed when they do.* The greater the pain people experience from dashed hopes, the greater fear they have of disappointment. As you encourage an atmosphere of hope in your group, be mindful that some members of your group may have experienced grave disappointments in their situations and relationships. Avoid letting people expect that the group will meet most of their critical needs. Know when to refer to a professional when people's needs exceed the ability of the group (see page 40-42, and 127 for help in knowing when to make a referral). Hope for change can be kept alive when adequate resources are brought into a person's life.

Fear of change. Even when life's circumstances appear unbearable, we often fear a change in those circumstances. This is because we are familiar, at least, with the difficulties we face. Familiarity brings a measure of stability and security, painful as things may be. In addition, change often brings additional pain and is sometimes frightening. We do not know what roles we should play, what to expect from others, or what ways to find comfort.

People overcome their fear of change when they observe others risking change and making it through safely. Encourage people to talk about their experiences of growth and change, including the fears and difficulties they faced along the way. These life experiences communicate, *You can do it. It may be difficult; but with the Lord's help, you can do it.*

Fear of failure. The fear of failure and its consequences may very well be the root of all our fears. No one wants to be a failure and to experience the resulting rejection by others. We want to be "somebody" and those who fail are "nobodies." At least this is what our culture teaches through the educational system and business activities. Encourage your group members that while we may experience failure, we are not failures as a result. In other words, who we are is not dependent upon what we do. When people place their trust in Christ alone for the forgiveness of their sins, they become children of God. That is who they are. Yet, Christians still sin and God still loves and accepts them (Psalms 51, 103; Romans 5:1-2; Hebrews 4:14-16; 10:17-22). Model this love and acceptance in your group, and you will help people overcome their fear of failure.*

Reasons why people join a group

In spite of their fears, people will still be motivated by personal needs to join your group. The elements of an effective small group environment listed above answer, in part, people's needs. The following list of motivations is partial but suggestive of some of the conscious and unconscious needs people bring to the group.

The need to belong. Life in the metropolitan centers of our country and the ease with which people change jobs and residences cause a lack of depth in people's roots in their communities. As a result, loneliness and feelings of estrangement can creep into people's lives. So people usually join a group in order to belong. In spite of their fears, they want to be known, loved, and appreciated for who they are. Even people who have healthy family relationships desire to belong to a group of peers outside the family. They want to be part of a community.

Oftentimes, however, people are afraid to let people into their lives so they can be known and loved. They may have been hurt or seen others hurt. They are afraid of similar injury and, thus, protect

---

* Howard, Wally. *RAP*, Waco, TX; Word Publishing, Creative Resources Division, 1972, pp. 75-78.

themselves by holding people at a distance until they can develop trust. They will still join a group seeking love and acceptance on an unconscious level. Since we have been created with a need to be loved, people overcome loneliness by becoming involved in various groups and activities. While few will outright say, "I'm lonely; please be my friend," many will carry an unconscious motivation of wanting to belong and be loved into their group membership. They want to be known, to be loved, and to be included for who they really are.

The need to contribute. People also need to love. As much as we are helped by knowing that others will be there for us, there is also great benefit in being able to help and support someone else. The benefit arises from the fact that as we help others, we are fulfilling our created design and that is satisfying (Galatians 6:2). Some people have become so dependent upon others' perceptions of their contributions that they are compelled to rescue and save almost everyone who crosses their paths. Yet, this aberration of our call to "share one another's burdens" does not nullify our need to be needed.

The need to understand. Many people who join a group need advice and help. A new perspective on life, its problems, promises, and rewards is all they need to lead their lives more effectively. Yet, many people are unaware of their need for new understanding. They may not join the group out of a conscious desire to gain insight into God and their own lives. Perhaps they may feel a general disquiet and discontentment with life; perhaps not. Yet, many people are encumbered with notions of what they should do and who they should be, which actually retards their spiritual and personal growth.

For example, a young mother of two preschool children may feel undesirable because of the effects of bearing and raising children upon her figure and grooming. She feels insecure in her husband's love even though he remains devoted to her. She may not join a group consciously seeking insight into her feelings of unworthiness. Nonetheless, she needs to understand God's acceptance of her, the proper basis of her image of herself. In addition, she needs insight into how she has built her self-worth upon the faulty foundation of her physical appearance. In short, whether or not people consciously recognize it, they need to understand the truth as revealed in God's word as well as the implications of that truth in their day-to-day lives.

Need to be understood. Not only do people need to understand, they need to be heard and understood. When they feel understood, they feel validated as a person of worth. For example, one young mother joined a grief support group after she had lost a child at birth. As she shared her experience of deep disappointment, confusion, and anger, the other members of the group responded with words like, "I know what you mean," "The same thing happened to me," and "I would feel the same if I were in your shoes." She felt understood and said, "I'm so glad to hear you all say these things. Before I came to this group, I felt like I was going crazy." She felt confirmed as a person with normal human responses at a time when she felt she was going out of her mind.

The need to regain control. If you are leading a group which offers the promise of recovery from some form of setback (for example, divorce, death of a family member, or chemical dependency), people will join out of a desire for help. They need the support of others to recover a normal life, and they are consciously looking for that support. By providing the elements of an effective group environment discussed above, you will be giving them the ability to regain control over their lives and start putting things back together.

Reasons why people lead a group

Many of the reasons that lead people to join a group also serve as motives for leading a group. Leaders also need to belong, contribute, understand, and regain control. Leading a group can fill these needs. We can help others as our own needs are being met. Yet, other motivations may also contribute to our desire for group leadership.

The search for significance. Some people lead groups out of a desire to feel important. For example, several college students began leading their own small group studies on eschatology, the doctrine of the last days, the "hot topic of the day." They later realized that they had unconsciously desired to be regarded as the "fount of knowledge" on a particular subject. They gained a sense of significance in being sought after for their ability to quote Scripture and answer people's questions about an interesting topic. Others may wish to gain an inside track on church leadership, build a following of their own, or be viewed as a rescuer for people in trouble. These motivations reveal a basic need for significance which is being met through group leadership.

Guilt. Unfortunately, some Christian leaders motivate their followers through guilt. People are made to feel guilty for their failures and lack of virtue. They tend to measure people's spirituality via their degree of involvement in the ministry's programs. As a result, followers who desire to grow spiritually feel they must immerse themselves in ministry activities in order to absolve their guilt. If the leader highlights the small group ministry, these individuals will gravitate toward small group leadership.

Most people of goodwill express their desire to lead a group in terms of helping others. However, some of our unconscious motives may be less self-giving. Rarely can we claim completely pure motives in seeking to lead a group. Yet, we should all be aware of reasons which may lie in the back of our minds. In this way, we can minimize our using others to accomplish self-centered goals.

Understanding The Role of Emotions

The issue of emotions and feelings will likely surface during the course of your group. If your group members apply the truth of Scripture into the deep corners of their lives with openness and honesty, the issue of emotions will arise. Yet, most evangelical Christians feel uncomfortable with discussions about and displays of emotions. This reservation is rooted in a proper concern that people place their faith in the Lord and in His moral guidance.

Through the entertainment industry and the educational system, our secular culture preaches, "If it feels good, do it," and conversely, "If it doesn't feel good, don't do it." Christians rightly should resist this teaching as a basis for godly living. In addition, God and His Word, not our emotional reactions to people and situations, are the only proper objects of our faith. Yet, many Christians have overreacted to our culture by disallowing emotions in the spiritual life. One leader observed, "In Christ I am a dead man; and dead men do not have emotions." Many who follow this dictum deny their negative emotions and, consequently, become emotionally numb to pain and also to joy.

Emotions are okay

Emotions do occupy a legitimate role in the Christian life. King David observes, "Surely you desire truth in the inner parts; you teach me wisdom in the inmost place" (Psalm 51:6). God wants us to be honest with what we experience deep inside us. This includes our thoughts, motives, and feelings. He desires that we deal honestly and truthfully with our emotions. In addition, we find the psalmist expressing his emotions to God as he struggles with life's circumstances. For example, David, "a man after God's own heart" (Acts 13:22), expressed his emotions to God by repeating four times the phrase, "How long?" as he waited for God's answer to his prayer (Psalm 13). He was hurting emotionally and expressed it to God. Yet, he continued to trust in God's goodness, "I will sing to the Lord, for he has been good to me." Faith and the expression of negative emotions can go together.

For the Christian, emotions should not be the object of his trust. They do not lead the believer. Rather, painful emotions indicate that something is amiss. For example, if one is fearful, he should not trust his fearful emotion. Instead, he should acknowledge his fear and examine the reasons for his fear. The fear indicates that something is wrong in his response to his situation.

Dealing with emotions

You can properly handle your emotions as a Christian by implementing the following suggestions.

a) Identify how you truly feel about the situation you face. You may generally feel uncomfortable in a particular situation. You will benefit greatly if you can identify your specific feelings. For example, your general discomfort may specifically be fear or anger. Allow yourself to experience the emotion. Do not bathe yourself in fear, for example, but do allow yourself to be afraid. In doing so, you take responsibility for the fact that you are indeed fearful. You will be less likely to deny your fear and deal untruthfully with your "inner man."

One way you can identify your emotions is through the kind of reflective prayer we read in the psalms. The psalmists descriptively recount not only their situations but their emotional reactions to those situations. Their poetry serves as a model for us as we deal with negative emotions.

b) Identify the thoughts that generate your feelings. Feelings do not occur in a vacuum. They emerge from our belief systems through which we interpret our life experiences. This is why two people can experience differing emotions as they encounter the same situation. For example, you may believe that those who fail should be rejected. Consequently, you experience fear of rejection when you show up late for work.

c) Gain God's perspective about your situation. Determine His view of who you are and what you are experiencing. Then trust Him by believing His Word instead of the elements of your belief system. For example, trust God when He says you are completely accepted by Him (Colossians 1:21-22) even though you show up late for work.

d) Finally, trust God to change your emotions. Often our emotions change, not instantly, but over a period of time. Allow yourself time to adjust and lean upon God's resources as you wait on Him to change you.

Scaling the "Ladder" of Intimacy

As you prepare for your group, you should be aware that people rarely communicate on the same level of intimacy with everyone they know. In fact, one might say we scale a ladder of openness and honesty in our relationships.

The first level or step is that of casual conversation, chitchat. Examples are "Hi, how are you?" "Boy, it sure is raining today" and "This line is slow, isn't it?" The depth of intimacy approaches that found in elevator talk.

On the second step, we exchange facts regarding what we know. Men's conversations around the office water cooler often reflect this level. "The Cards are doing poorly in the pennant race," "The price of stocks is down," "The 1950 Chevy sure is a classic car," are examples which occur on the fact exchange level.

An exchange of ideas occurs on the third step. On this step, we feel secure enough to tell what we think. Either we have done our homework and are able to defend our ideas, or we know the person we are talking to is not going to discount our input. Many solid friendships between American men are built on this level.

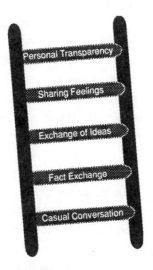

The Ladder of Intimacy: *Each rung up the ladder represents deeper, more transparent communication, though each step is shared with fewer and fewer people.*

On the fourth step, we share how we feel on a wide range of issues. It goes beyond the she-makes-me-so-mad often heard in the work place to sharing an I-feel-depressed-today type of disclosure. Women often build friendships on this level; men less often.

On the top step of the ladder is the exchange of dreams, hopes, fears, and failures. Personal transparency leads to a sense of being known for who you really are. True intimacy lies at this level. Sadly, many marriages lack this level of communication.

The climb up the ladder requires a trust that overcomes the fear of exposure and time in which to build that trust. Additionally, the higher you climb, the fewer people there are with whom you are able to share that level. We all share the level of "fact exchange" with scores of people. Yet, the time required to develop higher levels of intimacy limits the number of people with whom you can share your emotions and hopes.

People use this ladder in their interaction in your groups in three ways. First, people rarely begin their group interaction on the fourth step. People often need time to warm up to a disclosure of emotions. Early in the life of your group, people will interact mostly on the lower levels of intimacy, exchanging facts and ideas along with a few emotions. As the weeks progress and trust grows, people will interact more on the higher steps. In addition, people will begin each week on the lower steps and move up the ladder as the meeting proceeds. The more mature the group, the more quickly people move to the higher levels of interaction.

Second, people also need variety—maintaining a high level of intimacy in a group is emotionally taxing and uncomfortable. So, vary the levels of sharing you request of people via your discussion questions.

Third, people differ in their ability to climb the ladder. Men typically do not feel comfortable above the level of idea exchange. Others may desire to remain on the level of facts. Gently encourage people to move up the ladder, but do not force them to disclose more of themselves than they wish. Provide a safe environment for them in case they decide to climb higher than they have previously attempted.

Evaluation Questions

1. Think back upon the last group of which you were a member. At which stage did the group function most of the time?

   ❑   Stage One: exploration

   ❑   Stage Two: transition

   ❑   Stage Three: working

   What do you think kept the group at that stage?

   What could have been done to encourage the group to move to the third stage?

2. Which of the three stages of a group leader's development apply to you?

   ❑   Stage One: Focus on Self

   ❑   Stage Two: Focus on Content

   ❑   Stage Three: Focus on People

   How long have you been in that stage? Have you ever gone through all the stages?

What can you do to move to the third stage?

3. How would you describe your understanding of emotions in the Christian life?

4. Review the elements of an effective small group environment listed below. Put a check mark beside the two elements you feel will be the easiest for you to establish.

✓ ✗

❏ ❏ Love and acceptance_____

❏ ❏ Safety and trust_____

❏ ❏ Empathy and comfort_____

❏ ❏ Hope and encouragement_____

❏ ❏ Power and control_____

❏ ❏ Openness and honesty_____

❏ ❏ Freedom of expression _____

❏ ❏ Information and perspective_____

Now, place an "✗" beside the ones you feel will be the hardest for you to establish. Lastly, for those elements you marked with an "✗," write down a couple of ways you can improve your ability to establish that element.

5. Rate yourself on the following group leader traits and skills.

low   high
1 2 3 4 5...............................genuineness

1 2 3 4 5...............................nonpossessive love

1 2 3 4 5...............................empathy

1 2 3 4 5...............................active listening

1 2 3 4 5...............................encouraging openness

1 2 3 4 5...............................facilitating

1 2 3 4 5...............................knowing limits

6. Of the reasons why people join or lead a group, which ones do you think apply to you? How do these motivations affect your ability to lead an effective group?

❏ The need to belong

❏ The need to contribute

❏ The need to understand

❏ The need to be understood

❏ The need to regain control

❏ The need for significance

❏ The need to resolve guilt

7. List the people with whom you share the higher levels of intimacy.
   • Third Level - Exchange of Ideas

   • Fourth Level - Sharing of Feelings

   • Fifth Level - Sharing of Dreams, Hopes, and Fears

   • What do you feel allows you to share these levels with these people?

   • What prevents you from sharing greater intimacy with others?

8. List the names of your group members. Beside each name, indicate the top two motivations which you feel may fuel their involvement in the group. What qualities about your group will help meet their needs?

_____

_____

_____

_____

_____

_____

_____

_____

_____

_____

4

HOW TO LEAD A 12-STEP GROUP

Objectives:
- to understand the particular style of the 12-Step approach;
- to provide clear direction for beginning a 12-Step group; and
- to help the leader overcome common problems in these groups.

Millions of people have been profoundly affected by 12-Step groups. Dozens of organizations (notably Alcoholics Anonymous, Adult Children of Alcoholics, Lion Tamers, and many others) employ this method of teaching, reflection, and interaction. Rapha provides 12-Step workbooks on the important issues of:

chemical dependency;
codependency;
anorexia;
bulimia; and
compulsive overeating.

Our workbooks have also been adapted to help people on a wide range of other types of emotional and relational problems.

Like our other small group materials, these 12-Step workbooks are designed to promote honest reflection about life's struggles and solutions in an environment of love and acceptance. The 12-Step approach, however, offers a somewhat unique way to deal with these issues.

Distinctives of the 12-Step Approach

One distinctive of 12-Step groups is that they allow people the opportunity to proceed at their own pace. Members of the groups typically share what they have learned since the last meeting, so one person may tell how he has wrestled with an issue in Step 2 while another may describe her journey in Step 7. One person may proceed quickly at one point while another may need more time to reflect on those same truths. This flexibility allows each member to personalize the content and the pace of involvement.

A second distinctive of the 12-Step approach is the comprehensive nature of the material. The 12-Steps have been accurately described as a "path of repentance" taking someone...

- from denial to realization of problems
- to a sense of responsibility for those problems
- to forgiveness, restitution, and reconciliation
- to a new lifestyle of healthy decisions and relationships

This comprehensive approach avoids the "hit or miss" methods that may be meaningful at a certain point but leave people "stuck" in the process of healing and development.

Practical Suggestions

Content

The actual content of 12-Step group meetings can be quite varied. As already mentioned, one of the most popular methods is to have each person share what he or she is learning. Then other people can comment and reinforce that person's progress. A second method is to teach and interact on specific topics such as forgiveness, control, hurt, anger, concept of God, etc. A third option is to have members open their 12-Step workbooks to a particular Step and all go through it together. Fourth, sometimes the group may need to have a business meeting. The content of that meeting will cover functional issues such as refreshments, collections, splitting the group if it grows too large, and other related topics.

Any of these four types of content can fit into the two following formats.

Format

Traditional Format

1. Quiet moment (1 min.)

2. Read Opening Group Remarks & Prayer (1 min.)

3. Read Rapha's 12-Steps (3 min.)

4. Welcome new members & guests (3-10 min.) (Ask new members to introduce themselves if they wish)

5. Introduce facilitator and/or speaker for the group (2 min.)

6. Pass collection and prayer basket (1 min.)

7. Announcements (1 min.)

8. Coffee break (5 min.)

9. Content for the week (45-60 min.)

10. Read "Declaration" (1 min.)

11. Close with the "Lord's Prayer" (1 min.) Stand and hold hands

Optional Format

1. Read Opening Group Remarks & Prayer (1 min.)

2. Read Rapha's 12-Steps (3 min.)

3. Welcome new members & guests (3-10 min.)

4. Introduce facilitator and/or speaker for the group (2 min.)

5. Coffee break (5 min.)

6. Pass collection and prayer basket (1 min.)

7. Announcements (1 min.)

8. Content for the week (45-60 min.)

9. Close with the prayer (1 min.)

Note: Please give a copy of this outline to all group leaders prior to starting the session. A group leader is any person you have asked to take part in the group session.

Opening Group Remarks

(To be read by the facilitator—or someone appointed by the facilitator.)

Hello: my name is _____ and I am your leader for tonight.

This group is a fellowship of Christians who share experiences, strength, and hope with each other so that we might solve our common problems and grow in Christ.

We recover by being honest with ourselves and others. We define honesty as "freedom from self-deception" based upon a sincere desire to recover. This desire to recover binds us together so that we become willing to admit our wrongs and deal with others as we would have them deal with us.

Before we begin our sharing, I would like for you to know that we keep everything said here tonight confidential and in this room. Please attempt to use "I" messages instead of "you" messages, as we refrain from giving advice. My role as facilitator is to guide our topic, question, or your story around this circle. I may find it necessary to move the conversation on in order that all may have time to share. We plan to close at _____, but in case we run over, feel free to leave.

Please remember that this is a non-smoking group and that you should refrain from smoking while on church grounds.

Let's pray: *Dear Lord, by coming together to share our pain, may we minister to each other as your Holy Spirit reveals truth and healing to each heart and mind. In Jesus' name we pray. Amen.*

Declaration

This declaration can be read during the group meeting. (See the traditional and optional formats.)

Because of Christ's redemption,
I am a new creation of infinite worth.

I am deeply loved, I am completely forgiven,
I am fully pleasing, I am totally accepted by God.
I am absolutely complete in Christ.

When my performance reflects my new identity in Christ,
that reflection is dynamically unique.

There has never been another person like me
in the history of mankind,
nor will there ever be.
God has made me an original, one-of-a-kind;
a special person.

Note: The facilitator should give a copy of this declaration to each person before it is read by the group.

Getting Started

Week One - Planning the Ministry

Meet with your church small group coordinator to review the program with him and determine the role you should play in this program. A good way to do this is to review together the following facilitator criteria:

- desire for ministry with recovering individuals;
- experience of personal recovery from addiction, eating disorder, or codependency, and/or experience in 12-Step groups. (If

recovering from chemical dependency or eating disorders, at least two years of recovery are recommended.)
- spiritually mature and willing to submit to the leadership of the church staff; and
- teachable spirit.

Identify potential co-facilitators as well as any other individuals who might be interested. A male/female team is recommended but not necessary for chemical dependency and codependency groups.

Determine when the group or groups will start and where they will meet.

Develop a strategy for publicizing the ministry to the church (refer to Week Two).

Week Two - Publicizing the Group

Place an announcement in the church bulletin.

Make an announcement from the pulpit. If possible, include a brief testimony by the facilitator which identifies the need and benefits of small groups.

Church-wide events can be scheduled to develop greater congregational awareness. Possibilities include:

- *The Search for Significance* video series;
- a panel discussion on dysfunctional families, addictions, depression, and related topics; and
- sermon topics relating to addiction, codependency, eating disorders, depression, or related issues.

Sample Pulpit Announcement

A new program will be implemented in our church within a few weeks for individuals and family members who are struggling with various forms of addiction, eating disorders, and codependency.

Through a system of small support groups, people will be able to share together in an environment of unconditional love, acceptance, and confidentiality necessary for recovery. Initial groups will be formed for persons struggling with chemical addictions and codependency.

The program has been developed by Rapha, the nation's largest provider of psychiatric and substance abuse therapy from a Christian perspective. Rapha will provide training and direction for our church to establish and maintain the small group program.

The details for these groups are found in the church bulletin.

Note: You may not want to start all of these groups at once, so tailor your announcement in paragraph one to cover only the groups you plan to start.

Week Three - Contacting Interested Individuals

Contact individuals who respond to announcements about the small group program.

Begin to develop a list of individuals to form the nucleus of each group. Based upon your situation, it would be good to have several individuals who meet the following criteria:

- in the chemically dependent group, sobriety of one year or more;
- in the anorexia, bulimia, compulsive overeating, or codependency groups, significant progress in setting healthy limits and developing healthy relationships;
- familiarity with a 12-Step program and personal application of the Steps;
- participation in a 12-Step support group;
- a burden for the small group program; and
- a commitment to attend every group meeting during the 12 week start-up phase.

These people will not be co-leaders of the group, but their progress will provide modeling and encouragement for others who are beginning their recovery process.

Week Four - Beginning Your Group

Your group may start small. As the word spreads, however, additional people will want to attend. View the initial group as an opportunity to learn and make necessary adjustments. Plan to add other groups as the leadership becomes available.

Contact your Rapha small group coordinator at the number listed in your packet of material. He is available to help you as you begin the program in your church.

Establishing Accountability

Begin a same-sex buddy system. People are more likely to apply what they learn and maintain their commitment to the group and to sobriety if they are encouraged by someone. Consider pairing people by the second or third week so they can pray for one another, encourage one another, and strengthen the relationships in the group.

Also, encourage group members to select a temporary sponsor until they are able to choose a permanent sponsor. These sponsors may be found in the groups or other community groups. Each person, then, would have a buddy and a sponsor. A sponsor is someone who:

- has a sponsor of his or her own;
- has been in the recovery process for approximately two or more years;
- is a role model for recovery ;
- guides the group member through the 12-Steps;
- is a friend and a source of loving support; and
- understands and respects the principle of anonymity.

An effective sponsor:

- will not give advice, rescue, or fix the group member;
- will not act as a therapist;
- will not break anonymity by sharing confidences with others;
- will not give harsh or shaming criticism; and
- will not neglect his or her own personal recovery in order to attend to the group member's needs.

Sharing leadership provides an opportunity for all the group members to feel ownership of the group and, therefore, feel accountable to the group and responsible for its ongoing success. It is important to delegate part of the leadership team. After all, each member's recovery is at stake if the group should fail.

Group Distress Signals

The following situations can prove a real challenge to the facilitator. They are explained on the following pages.

- No one will talk.
- A group participant argues on a consistent basis.
- A group participant comes to the group obviously inebriated or under the influence of drugs.
- The group leader starts feeling anxious, angry, codependent, or "burned out."
- It becomes evident that confidentiality has been broken.
- Group participants become romantically attracted to each other, appropriately or inappropriately, and this comes to the attention of the group leader.
- A group participant, very early in recovery, decides to start his own ministry to help other addicts.
- A group participant insists that he/she doesn't need to do all of this "12-Step stuff" because Jesus has brought about the cure.

Now let's look at each of these in more detail.

1. *No one will talk.*
    Sometimes people in the group are unwilling to discuss what they are thinking or feeling. There may be many reasons for this. Perhaps the trust level has not developed in the group. People may fear that what is shared will be disclosed outside the meeting. Maybe everyone has just had a hard day and wants to listen. Rather than "force" the group, you may consider the following:
    - Check with the group to see if any of the reasons mentioned above are true.
    - Offer to pray for the group, and then just have a "step study." In a step study, each person reads a paragraph or two from the workbook. Discussion is allowed, but not necessary. These groups can be restful and can lead to greater group cohesiveness.
    - Consider playing a tape of a recovering person, or playing a tape on *The Search for Significance.*

While these alternatives are not to be used often, they occasionally provide relief.

2. *A group participant argues on a consistent basis with what other people in the group are saying.*

At the beginning of the meeting, it may be necessary to encourage people to share their own experience, strength, and hope and not to comment or criticize other participants' experiences and beliefs. It is important for you to let the group know that they do not need to agree with each other on everything. They need only be willing to work the 12-Steps and look inside their own hearts.

If this situation persists, it may be necessary to discuss the problem with the church coordinator of Right Step or the pastor. Usually when someone is very argumentative, he or she is feeling threatened. While this person may need special attention, it is unwise to sacrifice the entire group.

3. *A group participant comes to the group obviously inebriated or under the influence of drugs.*

The level of intoxication will determine how you should handle this kind of situation. If the member is manageable, it would be wise to ask a co-facilitator or member of the core group to meet with him individually during the group time. Make sure that transportation is provided. This is an opportunity to plant seeds for intervention and intensive treatment. It may be that this is the time for professional help and the group member is ready. You should allow time for the group to process their own feelings about this incident. Typically, group participants will either be angry at the relapser or feel that they are at fault for not preventing the relapse. The fear that they, too, could relapse often underlies these feelings. End the group with prayer for the relapsed person.

4. *The group leader starts feeling anxious, angry/codependent, or "burned out."*

One of the most common experiences of both professional and lay persons in the field of chemical dependency and codepen-

dency is burnout. Chemically dependent and codependent people are typically very intense and needy, and it is easy to lose perspective when working with them. Signs of burnout include:
- persistent irritation and anger at small things;
- an overwhelming sense of need to caretake the addict/alcoholic;
- thinking obsessively about what has gone on in the groups;
- feeling hopeless;
- feeling personally responsible when someone has relapsed;
- feeling that you are the only one who can do this work; and
- sleep disturbance.

There are many other signs of this type of stress. It is important not to ignore them. The psyche is trying to say *Take a break!* Make certain that you stay in contact with the pastor and other support group leaders. It may be necessary for you to take a leave of absence from the group and let someone else lead for a while.

5. *It becomes evident that confidentiality has been broken. Other church members know what has been shared in the group.*
     Nothing is more destructive to a support group than gossip. Sometimes it is helpful to have each group participant verbally commit to the confidentiality of the group. The need to break confidentiality is usually an ego issue, resulting from a desire to show others that you are "in the know." This can be particularly deadly in church settings where such rationalizations as: "God told me to share it," or "I felt his wife had a right to know what he has been doing" can be common. If there is a significant confidentiality breach in the group, have a group topic on confidentiality. After such a breach, it will take time to develop trust again.

6. *Group participants are romantically attracted to each other—appropriately or inappropriately—and this comes to the attention of the group leader.*
     While other people's behavior cannot be controlled, it is appropriate at various times in the duration of these groups to talk

about what is called "13th stepping." This occurs when the chemically dependent or codependent person starts to focus on romantic or sexual feelings toward someone in the recovery group, rather than on his or her own recovery. When someone feels stronger emotionally, many intense emotions surface which may have been deadened for a while. It is natural to want to act on these feelings. However, within the chemical dependency and codependency treatment field, it is a rule of thumb to avoid making any major decisions during the first year of recovery. The first year should be spent focusing on recovery and helping others. It has been proven over the years that intense romantic involvements early in recovery, quick marriages, and divorces all take their toll on the recovering person. Often they lead to relapse. While the facilitator cannot force the person in the group to believe this principle, it is still wise to say it often.

7. *A group participant very early in recovery decides to start his own ministry to help other addicts or codependents.*

Encourage the participant to take the log out of his own eye before he tries to help other addicts or codependents recover. It is actually a form of denial to "carry the message" too soon. Working the steps and focusing on recovery should be primary. Even the Apostle Paul had to wait years after his Damascus Road experience before beginning his missionary work. Addicts, alcoholics, and codependents are no different. Confronting an addict or codependent who says he has a direct message from God can be a sensitive issue, however, the way he presents the message usually shows the attitude of his heart. He may be extremely intense or even hysterical.

8. *A group participant insists that he doesn't need to do all of this "12-step stuff" because Jesus has brought about the cure.*

Actually, this may be true. There are cases of this kind of deliverance documented through the centuries. We don't need to argue this point. Rather, the facilitator can inform the person that the focus of this group is renewal of the mind through the 12-Steps with Jesus Christ at the center. Whether or not the person chooses to take advantage of the group is his choice. It may take time for it to become clear whether this person has actually been delivered, or whether he is using hyper-religiosity as a form of denial, in which case relapse will probably occur. The important thing to remember here is that arguing will not work. The purpose of this group is to make the 12-Steps easily available as a tool for recovery.

Group Issues

The group dynamics which were discussed in the session on the Addictive/Dysfunctional Personality also apply to your codependency group. Please review them again with regard to beginning a codependency group. Here are additional issues to consider with codependency groups.

"Cross-talk"

Cross-talk occurs when individuals speak out of turn and interrupt one another. The group is disrupted, and it loses its focus of respect for the member whose turn it is to speak. Because these groups are so full of "caretakers," sometimes they can degenerate into rapid-fire discussions where the format can be lost. This is destructive to the very necessary structure of the group and is discouraged. Sometimes it may be necessary to emphasize this statement at the beginning of the discussion group: "Cross-talk is discouraged."

Lengthy talkers

When someone who has been in great emotional pain for some time finds a codependency group full of warm and caring persons, the relief is often so great that he wants to share all of his pain. While you will need to use discernment in each separate case, it can be destructive to the group to allow an entire group to be taken up with one person's pain. As the facilitator, let the Holy Spirit guide you in this meeting.

Sometimes is may be necessary to interrupt the person and say how glad you are that he came, and that it would be good for him to stay after the group and talk to some members. You need to move the group along so that everyone can have a chance to share. Since you have already expressed this in the reading at the beginning of the meeting, it will not be too great a surprise. Remember that people who are new to meetings are fragile emotionally, and it is important not to embarrass them.

At the same time, if one person is allowed to dominate, the group itself will disintegrate. Help the members stay within time boundaries by establishing a group policy that verbal domination isn't allowed. Lengthy self-searching is encouraged through taking a fourth and fifth step. The meeting needs to be focused on recovery, even as people are open and honest about their pain.

Excessive emotionality

Codependents have often denied their painful feelings for so long that starting to look at their pain is the equivalent of "breaking the dam" in terms of tears and painful feelings. While crying and expressing feelings in meetings is fine, it is important to continue with the group. Providing a kleenex or a gentle pat on the hand can be reassuring. For instance, say to the crying person, "Well, we're glad you're here and keep coming back; it'll get better." Then move on to the next person to maintain the group structure while acknowledging the person's pain and reassuring him that recovery is imminent.

The danger in these situations is less for the hurting person who is letting go of repressed pain, and more for the other codependents in the group who are triggered to try to "rescue" such a person. While it is important to care for persons in the group, it is important to emphasize that Christ is the healer and that each person has access to the healing. It is dangerous to do "caretaking" rather than "caregiving" in a situation like this.

Someone needs child care

No children should be allowed in the meetings. It can not only be detrimental for the child to be in an intense emotional meeting, but can also impede true sharing for other members. The group may decide to use part of the group treasury to pay for a sitter. New group members should be encouraged by telephone to find a sitter.

Giving advice

Caretakers tend compulsively to advise other hurting persons. However, real recovery comes not from receiving advice, but from being willing to surrender to the Lord, to work the 12-Steps, and to utilize other tools of recovery and renewal. It may be necessary to gently, but regularly, reinforce the fact that members are encouraged to share their own experience, strength, and hope, without giving advice to others.

Conclusion

Rapha offers basic group leader training, advanced training for more experienced leaders, and specialized video training for chemical dependency and codependency 12-Step groups.

We trust that this brief introduction to the 12-Step process will help you get off to a good start with your group. If you have any questions, please call Rapha's Small Group Hotline at 1-800-383-HOPE.

5

YOUR GROUP AS A FAMILY

Objectives:

- to understand how members of your group grew up in their families and how their backgrounds influence their group involvement; and
- to gain a perspective of how your group can function as the "family of God."

One young woman recently joined a mission organization upon her graduation from college. When she arrived at her ministry assignment, she said to her new collegues, "My parents neglected me while I was growing up. I have no brothers or sisters. You are the only people that matter to me. You are my family."

What this young missionary said of her relationship with her co-workers is true for all believers. The Apostle Paul explains that every Christian becomes a child of God and, hence, brothers and sisters of Christ (Romans 8:16-17, 21, 29). He also refers to the Christian community as the "the family of believers" (Galations 6:10). Peter, likewise, addresses his readers as the "the family of God" (I Peter 4:17). At the new birth (John 1:12-13) every Christian becomes a member of God's family and shares a family relationship with other Christians.

Yet, this young missionary's experience brings this biblical emphasis into sharper focus. Her family did not nurture her as she grew up. Sure, they fed, clothed, and housed her, took her to the doctor when she was sick, gave her presents at Christmas, and sent her to school. Yet, they did not care for her mentally, emotionally, and spiritually. So when she started life on her own, she looked to the family of God as her source of nourishment and care. She rightly believed that the family of God is a source of redemption for those who suffer from deprivation in their human families.

Dysfunctional Families

Sadly, like this young missionary, many people grow up in families which do not function in healthy ways. Their families do not allow a full range of normal human behaviors, emotions, and interactions for the adults or the children. In this sense, these families are dysfunctional; they do not function as they should. Researchers have noticed certain patterns of behavior in the dysfunctional families they study. Greater levels of family dysfunction occur when these patterns are dominant. Chief among these patterns is the communication of a predictable set of messages.

Do not feel

Dysfunctional families do not allow children to feel. Either through a lack of modeling of proper emotional behavior or through punishment for any display of emotions, dysfunctional families do not allow their children to feel their emotions. For example, a child who grows up in a home where his parents do not express any emotion, negative or positive, will have great difficulty in dealing with his own emotions. Additionally, if a child is consistently punished when he displays anger, for example, he will learn to repress any angry feelings he encounters as an adult. Many adults experience great difficulty with their emotions because during childhood they heard such refrains as, "Big girls don't cry," "Don't be a sissy, son; quit crying," or "You shouldn't feel that way."

Do not trust

Children from dysfunctional families do not learn to trust. Children cannot learn trust in an unstable environment. The instability may be caused by the father's chronic job changing, by a serious illness of a parent, or by a parent's drinking behavior. Divorce, emotional and legal, also creates instability for a child. In addition, some parents simply neglect their children by not caring about how they get home from school, whether they stay out late at night, or what kind of friends they have. Simple gestures can teach a child to trust or not to trust. For example, if a father forgets a promised trip to the playground and makes no effort to make it up, his children learn to distrust their father's word.

Do not talk

Those who grow up in dysfunctional families learn to not talk. Any group of people living together must talk, but they may talk on a superficial level only. In dysfunctional families, children are not allowed to express in words what they think or feel. They certainly are not allowed to talk about the real problems the family may face. For example, if a family is evicted from their apartment because the father has gambled away the rent check, the children are not likely to be allowed to point out the problem (Dad). They may be allowed to talk about the weather as they watch their belongings soak up the rain on the sidewalk. But family rules do not allow anyone to criticize Dad. If someone does criticize him, he is quickly censured.

Many parents teach their children not to talk by such comments as, "Children should be seen and not heard," "I didn't ask you what you think; just do what I said," or "Don't talk back to your father."

Do not touch

Finally, dysfunctional families do not allow children to touch appropriately. Some children are touched only when they are being spanked or physically abused. Others are simply never cuddled by their parents. Still others never see their parents hug or kiss. These children do not learn to touch appropriately. Many American men are taught while growing up that men do not touch (unless while shaking hands, playing contact sports, or seeking sex). Thus, they have trouble expressing affection both to women and other men. Many girls are sexually abused, either through the acts of a stranger or, more likely, through incest. They also have great difficulty expressing affection; they are unsure of what constitutes proper touching.

Your Group as a "Family of God"

Dysfunctional families produce adults whose inability to feel, talk, trust, and touch appropriately will affect the dynamics of your group interaction. Yet, you can help these people by allowing your group to function as the family of God.

Allow people to feel

Effective small groups focus not only upon ideas but on how people feel about those ideas. It is one thing to say, "God loves me" (an idea); it is quite another to say, "I feel secure because God loves me." The heart-felt application of the latter statement should characterize your group discussions. When people begin to express emotions in your group, beware of others who may feel uncomfortable with emotions. They may attempt to solve the person's problem and thereby remove the reason for their feelings. Or they may overtly say, "You shouldn't feel that way."

For example, Thomas, a young father of three, talked to a friend about his emotional struggles. As his friend allowed him to talk about how his difficulties affected him, Thomas began to cry. Another friend standing nearby felt uncomfortable and jumped into the conversation, offering advice and perspective. Almost immediately, Thomas distanced himself from his feelings and the conversation soon ended.

The advice offered by the mutual friend was biblical and the perspective helpful. But it was offered too soon. Thomas was robbed of the chance to use his feelings as a gauge of his personal belief system. In light of the quick advice, he reasoned that he had no just cause to feel discouraged and depressed. He was not allowed to feel.

He lost the chance to use his feelings as a window into what he really believed about God and His provision.

Help people to learn to trust

By displaying the love and acceptance of God to your group members, you will provide the safety they need to learn to trust. Be consistent and maintain confidentiality. Do what you said you would do (e.g. start and end on time, cover a certain topic, return to a person's question, etc.) and let people tell their own stories. An environment with these elements of safety builds trust.

Michelle grew up in a legalistic Christian home. As an adult, she continued to worship in a rules-oriented church. Yet, she rarely felt accepted or loved in this community. She could not trust anyone out of a fear of failing to meet up to the strict expectations of her friends at church. After a few years, Michelle began to attend a church where people did not condemn others for their failures and she began to experience the forgiveness of God. She became a more open person as she began to develop relationships based upon trust.

Encourage people to talk

Good questions do more than provide for a good group discussion. They allow people the chance to express their ideas and thoughts. When you listen, you communicate that what others say is important. More importantly, you affirm that people are important, that they matter. Keep in mind that conversation and discussion have differing degrees of value. Recall the ladder of intimacy from Chapter Three (see page 71). Many people from dysfunctional families can engage in the equivalant of elevator talk. They are also comfortable with an exchange of facts. But dysfunctional families produce people who fear talking about ideas, opinions, and dreams. They possess a reduced ability to talk about the real issues of life and faith. Yet, by encouraging good discussion in your group, you can help people move up that ladder of intimacy and talk about real issues and answers.

One specific way you can help people from dysfunctional families is to deal with conflict in the group. Most group leaders dread the day conflict surfaces in their groups. Yet, if you handle the conflict properly, you can model good communication. As people learn that they can express their ideas, disagree with other people's ideas, and still walk away friends, they will be better able to manage conflict in their marriages and work relationships.

Allow appropriate touch among your group members

Social norms define appropriate touch. Move beyond these boundaries only on rare occasions, if at all. Your modeling of proper touch can encourage appropriate displays of affection and compassion. Exercise caution when encouraging touch. Do not force people to touch others. Beware of your own need for touch and using your group to meet that need. For example, having group members hug the person next to them out of your need to hug and be hugged is dishonest.

In short, you can create an environment in which people from dysfunctional families can learn to enter into healthy relationships. You can help others heal the hurts in their own lives (and we all have hurts). You can also help them raise their own children or grandchildren in a biblical way.*

*For further discussion of families and how family members interact with one another, see Chapter Six.

Evaluation Questions

The members of your group will bring emotional, spiritual, and relational "baggage" from their backgrounds into the group meetings. Their sense of compulsion, denial, guilt, shame, anger, hopelessness, loneliness, and other characteristics are often traced to relationships in their families, including other past and present relationships.

It is no surprise that you bring some baggage, too. Sometimes a group member may treat you the way a hurtful parent or sibling treated you. Then, instead of responding to the situation with objectivity and healthy detachment, you find it easy to react to that group member in the same way that you have reacted to your parent or sibling.

We want you to be aware of the dynamics of past relationships in your life so that you can anticipate how you can respond positively to the people in your group. These questions are designed to help you analyze your family and its effects, both positive and negative, on you.

Family Analysis

1. What were the strengths and weaknesses of your family when you were growing up?

2. Were any of these characteristics present in your family?

Addictions:
- ❏ problem drinking
- ❏ drug addiction
- ❏ eating disorders
- ❏ sexual addiction
- ❏ other addiction

- ❏ alcoholism
- ❏ workaholism
- ❏ gambling addiction
- ❏ success or money addiction

Other dysfunctional characteristics:

❏ divorce

❏ "smothering by parent"

❏ emotional abuse

❏ sexual abuse

❏ domineering father/passive mother

❏ domineering mother/passive father

❏ constant tension/anxiety

❏ neglect

❏ verbal abuse

❏ physical abuse

❏ psychosomatic illness

❏ loss of memory

❏ depression

❏ other_____

3. Describe your relationship with your father (pros and cons).

4. Describe your relationship with your mother (pros and cons).

5. Describe your relationship with each of your siblings (pros and cons).

6. Describe how these relationships affected you regarding:

a healthy self-esteem .... anger
experiencing forgiveness .... guilt
expressing forgiveness .... critical of others
love .... hate
accurate perceptions .... black and white perspective of
                                                                                people or situations
the ability to set limits .... being overly responsible
being responsible for your behavior .... irresponsibility
good bonding in relationships .... loneliness
free to express your feelings,
       ideas, decisions .... being a puppet/people pleaser
ability to have fun .... stiff or depressed
ability to talk, feel, and trust .... repressed emotions/explosions
                                                                                of anger

7. What strengths have been built into your life as a result of your family background?

8. What weaknesses or needs have developed in your life as a result of your family background?

9. How will these strengths and weaknesses affect your leadership/ relationships with people in the group? (How will you respond when people dominate, withdraw, disagree, fawn over you, etc.?)

10. What have you learned about yourself and your family from this analysis?

11. How can you be better prepared to lead your group in light of this analysis?

PART II
THE MEMBER'S GROWTH

6

FAMILY SYSTEMS

Objectives:
- to provide a deeper understanding of how the family environment profoundly affects each person in the group;
- to explain common behaviors and emotions of those from dysfunctional families.

As we learned in Chapter Four, a person's relationship with his family profoundly affects his perceptions and growth. In this chapter, we will expand on those issues by examining the functional family system, the dysfunctional family system, and characteristics of people from dysfunctional families.

The Functional Family System

When children are born into a strong and loving family, they become part of a "living organism" designed by God to provide a safe, nurturing environment to help children through their developmental phases. However, when any part of this family organism becomes afflicted with addiction, the entire organism is affected in the same way that an illness in your kidney will cause your entire body to become sick and dysfunctional. In order to describe the dysfunctional family, let's first look at what a functional family is.

A functional family isn't perfect, but it does offer a sense of unconditional acceptance of all its members. This unconditional acceptance does not imply a lack of discipline. Even during arguments or when discipline occurs, love and acceptance are at the core of the family. Family members can make mistakes and take risks without being ridiculed. They are able to *talk* together, to express *feelings*, to *trust* that they are accepted and that most of their needs will be met. In this kind of atmosphere, children receive adequate nurturing for their own growth. During their formative years, they are able to build what we call a positive self-concept.

The Dysfunctional Family System

In contrast to a functional family, a dysfunctional family follows three rules: *don't talk, don't feel, don't trust.*

In a dysfunctional family, there is a strong feeling among family members that something is wrong. There is a tendency to deny or disregard this feeling because it seems so overwhelming or threatening. Many parents in dysfunctional families come from dysfunctional families themselves, so they have very little experience talking, feeling, and trusting.

The ability to function well is learned behavior. Scripture tells us that the human heart—if left to itself—will move toward selfishness. Psychological studies support this truth. We must be taught to be open and unconditionally caring. In dysfunctional families, however, the development of openness and love is blocked. Denial of the problems in the family effectively cuts off objectivity and the possibility for change.

There are many types of family dysfunctions, such as addiction/ alcoholism, extreme parental emotional rigidity, sexual abuse, physical or psychological spousal or child abuse, eating disorders, chronic illness, divorce, etc. The results within the family system are often the same. Family members begin to move unconsciously into a

The Functional Family System*

survival mode. The following pages illustrate some of the differences between the functional and dysfunctional family.

When parents are healthy and create an environment of love, children can develop a positive self-concept. They are able to assume productive roles in society and meet life's challenges. The inner circles represent the development of a person's self-concept. The parents are represented as having healthy self-concepts which are indicated by the darkened inner circles. In the children, various degrees of shading are used to indicate development of the self-concept. The outer circles represent life roles. Examples of life roles include the following.

- Parent - wife, mother, teacher, friend, artist
- Parent - husband, father, businessman, friend, Sunday school teacher
- Child - brother, sister, student, athlete, dancer, friend

The Dysfunctional Family System*

In the dysfunctional family system, the primary goal of family members is survival. Children experience very little development. They assume rigid roles and don't develop a healthy sense of self-esteem. As a result, they are doomed to continue playing out the survival roles of their youth in their marriages, families, and other relationships. In this type of family system, most normal self-development is lost. All of the unconscious focus is on the dysfunctional person.

- The **Enabler** tries to make everything okay.
- The **Hero** thinks that by being perfect, he can cause the addiction to go away.

* Adapted from *The Family Trap* by Sharon Wegscheider-Cruse.

- The **Scapegoat** rebels against family problems and ultimately believes that he himself is the problem.
- The **Lost Child** pulls into a shell, withdraws, and isolates himself from meaningful relationships.
- The **Mascot** tries desperately to make everyone laugh in the midst of the tragedy of the family situation.

Children in these systems rarely build healthy self-concepts. They are at great risk for multiple marriages, addiction, codependency, mental illness, and stress-related physical problems.

A person's emotional, relational, and spiritual growth can be blocked at any point in the developmental process, but generally, the earlier it happens, the greater the damage. For example, if a person does not develop personal boundaries, he will almost certainly have problems in the adolescent and maturity stages. And a person who has had bonding problems will likely develop difficulties in all of the subsequent stages as well.

It is not the isolated, traumatic incident that is usually the most detrimental to human development, but the consistently subtle, yet extremely powerful message that says, in effect, "You aren't loved," "You aren't good enough," "I'm ashamed of you," "I don't value your feelings or opinions." A person who is steeped in this environment not only believes that something is terribly wrong with himself, but that all of these hurtful communications are "normal" and will never be any different. It is an insidiously powerful situation which is, unfortunately, common to many. Parental modeling is among the most influential in human development. The way parents use their authority contributes either to a child's health and stability, or to his insecurity and instability.

It may be important to emphasize here that our goal in presenting this material is not to blame others, but to understand how people develop healthy self-concepts and relationships, and what may have hindered this process in some of our lives. Understanding these issues may prove to be painful, and we may realize some unpleasant things about our parents, but understanding is not the same as condemnation. In a later chapter we will see how important it is to forgive those who have hurt us. At this point, we simply are trying to see if and how we have been hurt.

Let's examine the causes and symptoms of hindered or reversed growth in the developmental stages of bonding and separateness:

When Development Is Blocked in the Bonding Stage

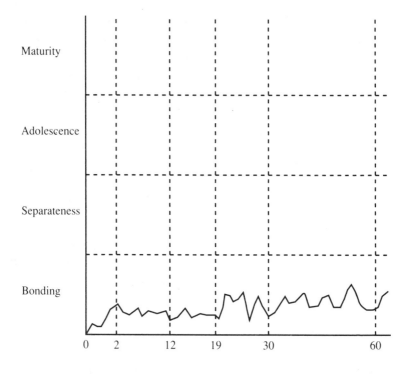

One of at least three significant events occurs in the life of a child during the bonding stage: he or she develops an attachment to a loving role model; he or she develops an attachment to an abusive role model; he or she is unable to form a significant bond with a role-model figure. The absence of bonding presents tremendous problems in every area of human development. For example, one woman I counseled was raised by emotionally troubled parents. They became so absorbed in their own personal and relational problems that they had no time or energy left to give her. They lived together in the same house, but emotionally, her parents were absent.

As another example, a young man I know has an alcoholic father and a demanding, manipulative mother. His father spent very little time with the family, and his mother expected her young son to meet the emotional needs her husband failed to meet. In response to her demands, his primary concern became pleasing his mother and trying to win her approval. He consequently developed an unhealthy bond with his mother and had problems establishing limits, or a sense of separateness from her and others. The result was a rescuing, codependent relationship with his mother, which carried over into all of his relationships.

Bonding problems primarily result from abandonment (physical and/or emotional neglect) and abuse (emotional, physical, sexual, verbal, etc.). The symptoms manifested by those who have not experienced a deep sense of being loved and valued are tragic, especially when contrasted with those which result from healthy bonding. Here are some of them:

Results of Healthy Bonding	Results of Bonding Problems
loved	self-hatred
lovable	shame, depression
value, worth	emptiness
valuable	often, addictions to drugs, alcohol,
closeness	success, pleasing people, food, etc.
intimacy	fear of closeness, fear of being known,
	loneliness, denial, the inability to
	perceive and experience reality,
	feeling attacked (often because of
	the reality of being attacked),
	anxiety, fear

All of us exhibit some negative feelings and behaviors from time to time, but not to the extent that those with bonding difficulties do. As I explained these stages at a seminar, one woman commented, "I have felt lonely. Do I have bonding problems?" After more discussion, I explained that a person who is stuck in the bonding stage often has a pervasive and oppressive sense of loneliness (if he is in touch with his emotions). It is not a temporary feeling.

When a person's development is blocked in the bonding stage, it is often quite difficult for him to believe that God or anyone else could possibly love him. But a compounding problem is that he often doesn't even know what love is. He is then unaware of the nature and depth of both his need and the defense mechanisms he has unconsciously incorporated to block his pain.

When Development Is Blocked in the Separateness Stage

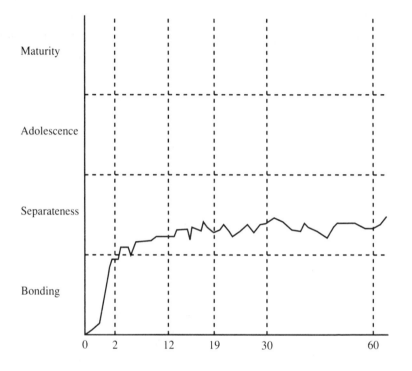

Establishing boundaries during the stage of separateness is much like setting physical boundaries on a piece of property. The idea is that if each of us owned a ranch, we would individually be responsible for setting its boundaries, and then caring for it and protecting it. As caretakers, we also would be responsible for choosing whom to allow on our property. If invited to another person's ranch, we could visit, though we would not try to run anyone else's ranch, nor would we allow anyone else to run ours.

In the same way, we have individual personalities (thoughts, feelings, and behavior), and we are responsible for setting our personal boundaries. We should establish what about ourselves we will share—and with whom. We may choose to allow certain others to share themselves with us. But we must avoid trying to run other people's lives, just as we should not allow others to run ours.

The desired result of the bonding and separateness stages is a healthy independence of one's self, not selfishness; a recognition of one's individuality, not isolation or self-indulgence.

A dysfunctional person, however, doesn't "stay on his ranch." He goes over to others' ranches to farm the crops, live in the house, and tend the cattle. If the other person is needy, such as an alcoholic, he may at first welcome the intrusion of the overly responsible "caretaker." Others, however, may deeply resent this kind of meddling on their turf. And usually, even the addictive, needy people will begin to resent his "help."

While he is taking care of someone else's ranch, he neglects his own. He doesn't cultivate strength and stability in his own life because he's too busy strengthening others. He probably doesn't even realize his own ranch (his emotions, desires, behavior, attitudes, etc.) is being neglected. He only knows that he's doing the best he can do, and he sure hopes that other people appreciate his hard work and sacrifice for them.

This ranch metaphor has been very helpful to me. I can visualize myself in years past hiding down among the cottonwoods in the creek bed because I had let some people burn my barn, steal my cattle, and ruin my crops. Others had come on my ranch to fix it up, paint the house, and hoe the garden. And I would often leave the cottonwoods to go to someone else's ranch to take care of their needs for them. Detaching helped me break my habit of ranch-hopping.

Detachment involves stepping away in order to be more objective and to make good decisions. We can learn to detach emotionally even when we are in a difficult situation or with someone who has controlled or condemned us. But sometimes we need to detach physically, to separate ourselves from someone who has dominated us. This separation gives us some "breathing room" and an opportunity to develop strength, stability, and a sense of confidence. We can relate to the person with more maturity the next time we are with him.

We can take a drive, go to the library, or take a walk for a while. We can take a couple of days from time to time to replenish emotional reserves and regain a sense of separateness and identity. We can take a sabbatical from a relationship (such as not calling a parent for a month or more). The type of physical detachment depends on such factors as: the type of relationship (spouse, child, parent, friend, employee, etc.), the level of need in your life, and the level of control exercised by the other person. I am not advocating a permanent physical separation (like divorce). Talk to a wise friend or counselor who can help you determine the best plan.

Physical detachment is, then, an aid to help develop strength and perception so we can more easily detach emotionally whenever we need to do so. All of us need to learn to detach emotionally and remain objective in the middle of conversations and situations. Many of us also need to detach physically. What kind of detachment is appropriate for you?

As Sharon, a woman I worked with, described her present life and family background to me, I noticed that she seemed to have a problem in determining what her responsibilities were. She tried to take care of others' problems, but she didn't do a very good job of solving her own. In fact, she expected others to take care of her problems for her. When others wouldn't or couldn't do so, she thought they were being selfish. She spent her life fixing up other people's "ranches," and she expected others to take care of hers.

Some people come on our ranches to fix them up. They give us "helpful advice." They make our decisions for us. They "serve us" tirelessly. Some may say that they are "just trying to help" us, but they may condemn and belittle us in the process so that we will say and do what they want. Both kinds of people come on our ranches to manipulate and control us. One tries to control through kindness; the other, through condemnation.

Parents often are unable to find a healthy balance between advising and correcting their child, and giving him the freedom and affirmation he needs to assume his own thoughts, feelings, and identity. They may offer the child a lot of nurturing as an infant, but by failing to teach him how to make his own decisions and take on those traits that are part of his unique personality, they fail to help him move from bonding to separateness. Their form of love is sustaining to the development of an infant, but smothering to a child in grade school, and even more harmful to the child who is growing into adolescence.

Most parents lean toward one end of a spectrum. Some are highly controlling, refusing to allow their children to work through the process of making their own decisions and developing their own thoughts and feelings. Other parents are relatively uninvolved in this important childhood process, so that their children have to try to figure things out entirely on their own. Both smothering and neglect create problems with the development of healthy independence for children. Some of these problems include:

- feeling responsible for making others happy, successful, and good;
- assuming others' thoughts, feelings, and behavior instead of developing one's own;
- being unable to say no without feeling guilty;
- saying yes to please others and win their approval;
- being manipulated (controlled) by others;
- trying to manipulate others;
- being unable to make decisions because of a fear of rejection or failure;
- having difficulty distinguishing between good and bad, acceptable or unacceptable behavior
- impulsively making decisions by perceiving different factors as "black or white," with very little ambiguity, or shades of gray (People and situations are seen as all good or all bad.);
- rescuing, fixing, enabling (codependency);
- being overly responsible/competitive;
- being irresponsible/passive;
- frequently demonstrating anger, bitterness, resentment; and
- living in denial, unable to see reality.

Again, the ranch illustration can help us see some of these difficulties. A person who has problems with establishing limits goes onto other people's ranches and makes decisions for them, while he lets them come onto his ranch and make his decisions for him. He jumps his fences and lives on somebody else's ranch (telling others how to think, feel, and act) while he lets others tell him how to do those things. He may get angry if they become too bossy or domineering, but he won't tell them to leave. After all, he's busy tending to somebody else's business.

Many people with separation difficulties actually have set limits—very rigid limits—in one or more specific areas of their lives. These might include raising their children or managing their job, their finances, or certain relationships. They may let others tell them what to think, feel, and do about many other parts of their lives, but not this one! If they feel threatened in this area (and they often do), they will defend it with tenacity and vengeance, often using either passive or aggressive behavior to do so.

John typifies those who have problems with setting limits. John's father believed that raising children was a woman's job. Therefore, he poured most of his time and energy into his work, so that he had very little of either left to give to his son or his wife. John's mother was a domineering woman who was accustomed to getting her way in the home. She usually did so by alternately giving and withholding praise and approval, by feigning illness, or by using sex as a tool for manipulation with her husband.

When John was growing up, he was rarely given opportunities to make his own decisions, and when he was, he often felt as though he'd been placed in a double bind. His mother might give him options, but she would withhold affection from him when he chose to do something that she really didn't want him to do. Rather than rebel, as some in similar situations do, John learned how to "read" his mother well and became devoted to making her happy in all that he said and did.

John was an exceptionally bright student who excelled in math and science. He made an independent decision to pursue a pre-med college program, and upon graduation, was accepted into medical school. He later started a private practice and married a woman much like his mother. When he married, John transferred his devotion and approval-seeking skills to his wife. He allowed her to run their home, to raise and discipline their kids, to tell him how to dress, how to drive, how he should feel, and what he should think. But if she tried to give him any input on how to run his practice, such as how he should deal with his patients or his secretary or nurse, or how he could arrange his furniture or his files, he became very agitated. His response was either to argue with her defensively or to act as if he'd listened to every word—and then dismiss all that she'd said.

Throughout his married years, John poured almost all of his available time and energy into his practice, working late and remaining on call on most evenings and weekends. Helping his patients as he did gave John the feeling that he was a hero, despite the negative influence his wife's domination had on his sense of manliness.

John had allowed himself to be driven from most of his ranch, but he was still clinging to a shed (his medical practice) in the back forty. When he felt threatened by his wife's inquiries or suggestions about his work, he responded by being defensive or by withdrawing, pretending to hear her but shutting out her words.

Others who are defending an area of their lives may make demands, whine, complain, criticize, or condemn the one(s) posing the perceived threat. Or, they may have a black-or-white response, believing that others are for them or against them, and try to get others on their "side" (against the perceived attackers). Again, it is common for those who have problems with establishing and maintaining limits to tell others how to run their lives, and then to be offended when the advice is not taken. It is easy to be frustrated and angry with people who are so defensive, but we need to remember that the root of their defensiveness is hurt. Seeing them as hurting people who act defensively to avoid reinjury helps us to be compassionate toward them. If we also are defensive, it helps us understand why we feel and act the way we do.

All of us experience false perceptions to some degree. In dysfunctional families, however, these false perceptions are internalized to a much greater extent. Interpersonal, emotional, and spiritual conflicts in dysfunctional families produce intense pain, guilt, shame, manipulation, and addictive or compulsive behavior.

During the formative years, children from dysfunctional families assimilate these distorted perceptions—or *false beliefs*—as their core belief system. These false beliefs can be stated like this:

- *I must meet certain standards in order to feel good about myself.*
- *I must have approval of certain others to feel good about myself.*
- *Those who fail are unworthy of love and deserve to be punished.*
- *I am what I am. I cannot change. I am hopeless.*

Throughout the dysfunctional person's life, situations are is colored and distorted by the false beliefs. The result is ungodly behavior. The process works something like this.

Belief System Based on False Beliefs	→	Ungodly Thoughts	→	Painful Emotions	→	Ungodly Actions

We often interpret the situations we encounter through our beliefs. Some of our interpretations are conscious reflections; most of them, however, are based on unconscious assumptions. These beliefs trigger certain thoughts, which, in turn, stimulate certain emotions, and from these emotions come our actions. In order for an emotion to persist, our belief system must continue to produce certain thoughts. For example, we probably will not stay sad without continuing to think sad thoughts. Think of it in this way: Our minds contain deeply held beliefs and attitudes which have been learned through our environment, experiences, and education. These beliefs and attitudes produce thoughts which reflect how we perceive the events in our lives. These thoughts, then, combined with past experiences, relationships, and patterns of behavior, are often the source of our emotions, and our emotions are usually the launching pad for our actions.

Understanding ourselves and how we think can help us in two ways: we can learn how to manage our responses to current events, and we can learn how to experience healing from the damage of our past. Understanding that our thoughts are usually products of our beliefs gives us a tool for exposing those beliefs and identifying their source. False beliefs usually become stronger through time because false perceptions of the individual and his circumstances are increasingly distorted. These false beliefs form powerful strongholds which distort his sense of identity and diminish his self-esteem.

Characteristics of Individuals From Dysfunctional Families

Dysfunction occurs when a person's God-given needs for love and security have been blocked in a relationship with a dysfunctional person, resulting in a lack of objectivity, a warped sense of responsibility, being controlled and controlling others (the three primary characteristics), and anger, guilt, and loneliness (the corollary characteristics). This affects the person's every relationship and desire. His goal in life is to avoid the pain of being unloved and to find ways to prove that he is lovable.

Behaviors:
A Lack of Objectivity - The members of an addict's family (or virtually any dysfunctional family) believe that their family is "normal." They simply cannot recognize their unhealthy ways of relating to one another because they have never seen emotional and relational health. Also, coming to grips with the reality of pain, hurt, anger, and manipulation can be very threatening, so they deny that the problem even exists. So the pattern continues. Some dysfunctional people are very perceptive people. They have had to learn to "read" others very carefully so they can say and do the things that avoid conflict and win approval. Though they have learned to be very perceptive about some things, they still do not see the damaging ways that people in their family relate to each other.

A Warped Sense of Responsibility - Common synonyms for codependency are: rescue, help, fix, and enable. The codependent sees himself as a savior. He has a compulsion to help others, especially the emotionally sick and addicted people in the family. The addict (or other dysfunctional person) does not take care of himself, and he uses both self-pity and condemnation to evoke a response from the overly responsible codependent. The codependent is so busy taking care of others, however, that he neglects to care of his own life, to make his own decisions, and to determine his own identity and behavior. A hurting person wants to be loved and accepted, and he wants to avoid conflict; so he does whatever it takes to make other people happy.

Controlled and Controlling - Like everyone else, a hurting person needs love and respect, but having been deprived of these precious commodities, he determines to do whatever it takes to win the affirmation he craves. His means to that end is to make people happy. His chief fear is that people will be unhappy with him. Those around him quickly learn what his "buttons" are and how to push them. Skillful use of praise and condemnation manipulate him as artfully as a puppeteer manipulates a puppet. The way he is treated soon becomes the way he will treat others. Typically, if he has been controlled, he will try to control others.

In his attempt to control people, he usually falls into two extremes. On the one hand, he may try to "mother" people (in the negative sense of the word), and shape their opinions and habits by constant attention with both praise and criticism. He does not let them out of his sight for long. Or, on the same end of the scale, he may become like a dictator, barking orders and exercising his real or perceived authority in their lives. On the other end of the continuum is withdrawal. A person may become so tired of trying to control others or may feel so inadequate and worthless, that he believes no one will do what he wants them to do. His poor self-concept overcomes his desire to manipulate and he gives up.

Emotions:

Hurt and Anger - Addiction creates a family system that may include words of love and acceptance, but actions often hurt people deeply. Hurt and anger go hand-in-glove. Hurt is the result of not being loved, not being valued. It comes from feeling abandoned, used, and condemned. Anger is the reaction toward the source of the hurt. These painful emotions are not only products of the codependent's past, they are a part of his reality every day. The need to have a sense of worth leads him to try to rescue the one who has hurt him, but inevitably he gets hurt again and again. Sooner or later, he gets angry.

Guilt - Hurting people often feel guilty. They feel guilty for what they have done and have not done. They feel guilty for what they have said, have not said, felt and have not felt. They feel guilty for just about everything. Often such guilt produces feelings of worthlessness and shame.

A dysfunctional person gets his worth—his identity—from what he does for others. He rescues, he helps, he enables, but no matter how much he does for others, it is never enough. That is the trap of living in a dysfunctional family. He rescues, but he is rejected. Lacking objectivity, he concludes: *It's my fault. If I were a better person, they would love me.* So he spends his life trying to be good enough. He may take on the hero role trying to earn the love and acceptance he so desperately wants, but fears he never will have. He may begin to act frustrated and angry, developing an addiction or some other type of destructive behavior. In either case, he is haunted by the shame that he has not—or cannot—measure up.

Loneliness - Many people spend their lives giving, helping, and serving others. They may appear to be the most social people in the world, but inside they are lonely. Their attempts to please others by helping and serving are designed to win affection. Though they may occasionally see a glimpse of love and respect, it usually fades all too quickly. Then, thinking they have been abandoned by both people and God, they feel empty and companionless. They distrust authority, believing that anyone above them is against them, and they build elaborate facades to hide their painful feelings of loneliness.

All of us experience these characteristics to some degree, but a dysfunctional person's life is characterized by them.

Evaluation Questions

1. What principles from this section seem most helpful to you? Why?

2. What aspects of this section are confusing to you?

3. How will you get these clarified? (Who can you talk to? What books can you read?)

4. What specific points will you apply from this section? How will you apply these?

7

THE HEALING PROCESS

Objectives:
- to provide insight into the complexities of emotional wounds and resulting defense mechanisms;
- to explain the need of both grief and responsibility in the healing process; and
- to understand that several crucial elements are necessary to the healing process.

The process of emotional, spiritual, and relational healing can seem complicated and mysterious. We can easily feel lost and confused, wondering if we are making any progress at all. As you lead your group, be aware of these complexities so you can help them find direction and encouragement in the maze. To help make sense of these complex issues, this chapter will examine why people hurt, how hurting people act, how to get well, and elements which contribute to the process.

Why People Hurt

Many of us can identify the immediate reason we hurt emotionally: someone has ignored us, rejected us, or laughed at us; we feel ashamed because we've failed or we don't look attractive; we have made mistake after mistake and our lives are wrecks. Our pain, however, is often compounded and complicated by several factors, including;

- present offenses;
- past offenses (the deep wounds of neglect, abuse, and manipulation in dysfunctional families);
- established dysfunctional behavior patterns (using a variety of defense mechanisms to try to feed our craving for love and respect, yet avoid the pain of failure and rejection); and
- complicating consequences (caused by poor decisions: debt, strained or broken relationships, bitterness, etc.).

The pain we feel may be blunted by the numbness some of us use to block the pain, but for many of us, our present hurts are magnified by unresolved past wounds. An analogy of this is a broken arm. When a healthy arm is thumped, there may be slight pain but it quickly subsides. When a broken arm is thumped, however, the great amount of pain is way out of proportion to the little things. Many of us are like people with broken arms: little things hurt a lot—and big blows are excruciatingly painful.

How They Act

Common personality types

Understanding our personality type (our goals, desires, defenses, and ways of relating to others) can significantly help in the healing process. As we learn to identify patterns in our behavior, we can predict how we usually act in given situations. Then when we have identified our usual behavior, we can more readily *choose* how we will act. Personality theories are many and sometimes complex. For instance, most of us respond in certain ways to some types of situations, but quite differently in others depending on factors such as the nature of the relationship or the perceived level of threat or gain. Some common personality types are listed below.

- *Passive aggressive* - marked by hidden resistance to authority.
- *Dependent* - always looking to another to give direction and assume responsibility.
- *Compulsive* - excessive neatness, orderliness, and promptness; usually rigid and stingy.
- *Histrionic* - attention seeking and dramatic; usually overreact emotionally.
- *Narcissistic* - excessive self-centeredness which borders on self-love.
- *Avoidant* - aloofness and absence of personal relationships; probably excessive daydreaming.
- *Borderline* - unstable, constantly fluctuating mood. Might be said to have a "stormy" personality.
- *Paranoid* - continually suspicious and jealous. They see the worst in everything.

Common behavior characteristics . . .

In conjunction with personality types, it is very helpful for people to identify certain behaviors. This identification serves to give perception that these behaviors may be the product of past wounds or poor choices. Also, in the context of a group, the identification and disclosure of these behaviors lets others know they are not alone. This realization often leads to help for change and real progress. Several categories of painful or destructive behavior include anxiety, depressed moods, clinical depression, and extreme behaviors.

. . . which express anxiety
aggressiveness
defensiveness
excessive talking

unprovoked anger
argumentative speech
constant busyness
rapid speech
restlessness
confused speech
constant sighing
excessive bragging
exaggerating
self-centeredness
hysteria
inappropriate laughter

. . . which express a depressed mood

passiveness
quietness
uncertainty
lack of facial expression
lack of activity
fearfulness
lack of confidence
lack of motivation

. . . of clinical depression

loss of appetite
excessive sleeping
inability to sleep
fear of death
frequent crying
confusion
listlessness
loss of facial expression
long periods of motionlessness
morbid thoughts
expressed hopelessness
excessive worry
strong guilt feelings

physical complaints
delusional thinking
thoughts of suicide

... of extreme behaviors: antisocial, self-destructive, disoriented
fighting
drug or alcohol abuse
violent outbursts
isolation
sexual aggression
obsessiveness
irrational fear
hearing voices
hysteria or panic
euphoria
lawlessness
expression of open hostility
erratic thought patterns

When to refer

As people feel more comfortable and safe in our groups, they often come to grips with hurt and anger which have been buried for years. Sometimes, the nurturing environment of the group is not enough because the person is overwhelmed by these emotions. It is important to realize when a person needs more help than our groups can provide. Then, referral to a professional counselor is appropriate.

In many cases, the person can benefit from a Christian counselor. Talk to your pastor to get the names of counselors who are both thoroughly Christian and clinically astute. In some cases, however, someone in our groups may need hospital care. Treatment programs for psychiatric problems or substance abuse vary greatly from facility to facility. It is very difficult to compare programs without first gaining specific information. General impressions of a treatment center through advertising, general reputation, or casual word of mouth should not be the primary reason for choosing a treatment center.

If you have any questions, we invite you to call one of our assessment counselors at Rapha. The toll free number is:

1 (800) 383 - HOPE

How to Get Well

Grieving the loss

Almost twenty years ago, Elisabeth Kübler-Ross wrote a book about the process that terminal cancer patients experience as they come to terms with their disease. The process of coping with the physical disease closely parallels that of dealing with emotional difficulties. The authors of several books have used this process to describe how a person comes to grips with emotional trauma.

Effectively dealing with traumatic difficulties includes five stages: denial, bargaining, anger, grief, and acceptance.* This is not a push-button, 1-2-3 kind of process. A person may move quickly through one phase, but very slowly through another. And he may go back and forth from time to time, re-entering a stage he has already gone through as he becomes aware of other pains and hurts he has not previously seen. Generally speaking, however, a person will not progress to the next stage until he has more or less fully experienced that which he is in. The following diagram may be helpful.

Objectivity is the door which opens into the process. Acceptance is the door leading out of it and into health. In the middle are three vats, or containers, representing bargaining, anger, and grief. A person

---

*Elisabeth Kübler-Ross, *On Death and Dying* (New York: MacMillan Publishing, 1969).

will not progress to constructive anger until he is through with bargaining, and he will not experience grief until he has spent his anger. (This, of course, does not mean that the person does not experience anger or grief except in that phase. It only means that these emotions will be dominant during that time.) Let's examine each of these phases in further detail.

Denial

Earlier, a good deal of space was devoted to the issue of why hurting people live without objectivity, so we will here briefly recap the main points of that topic.

- We don't have a viable point of comparison to contrast pathological behavior with healthy behavior. We think our families, our circumstances, our thoughts, our emotions, and our behavior are "normal."
- We may have developed an unconscious defense mechanism of staying so busy that we don't have time to reflect and feel pain. Many of us are driven people; driven to accomplish our own goals, and those established by organizations, corporations, and others. This compulsion is a vain attempt to block pain and gain a sense of self-worth.
- Some of us have become passive and emotionally numb in our effort to block pain. We avoid decisions and relationships when the risk of failure and rejection seems too high. (Actually, most of us use some combination of compulsion and passivity in our attempts to cope with our pain.)
- Some of us are so crushed, so hopeless, so depressed, that we don't believe anything good can or will ever happen to us. We withdraw into a cocoon of morbid introspection and self-hatred.
- Some have been sheltered, protected from the pains and joys of life. One man said: "My parents didn't let me make any decisions. They always decided what I would do, where I would go, which classes I would take, which hobbies and sports I would be involved in—everything! They would say things like, 'We're not going to let you go out for football because you wouldn't be very good at it. You'd fail, then you'd be disappointed, and we'd be disappointed, too.' For

me, failure was pre-determined because I had absolutely no confidence in myself. I am shy, insecure, and afraid to try anything because I might fail and let people down. To me, the worst thing that can happen is my disappointing someone by failing."

- The pain of neglect or condemnation is so great for some people that they recoil at being loved by someone. "Affirmation hurts. Love is painful. I can't take it!" said one sad woman.
- Some of us have so much repressed hurt and anger that we lose our tempers fairly often. These explosions are unlike the productive expressions that we will examine later in this chapter. They are not the product of understanding and objectivity. This anger is just the "tip of the iceberg," and is coupled with guilt and self-hatred, not healing forgiveness and understanding. Some people may say, "I must be pretty far along in the process. I'm really in touch with my anger," but in reality, they haven't even started the process because they have yet to see the root cause of their anger.

Objectivity is the door which enables us to enter the process of healing. Understanding pathological behavior and seeing its cumulative effects in our lives can be shocking at first, but that realization is necessary to participate in the rest of the process.

Bargaining

When a person gets a glimpse of the effects of codependency and dysfunction in his life, he will often respond by trying to bargain with himself, his family, and God. Christy learned about dysfunctional families from a close friend, and quickly saw those painful effects in her own life. At the end of the conversation, she was desperate for an answer. She blurted out, "Then how can I get my father to love me?" Her friend explained, "That's the wrong question, Christy. It's not up to you to get your father to love you. He is responsible for that. It's up to you to be independent and secure in the Lord, whether your father ever loves you or not."

Bargaining takes many shapes and forms, but its goal is to get other people to change by offering some change in ourselves. *I'll be a better husband to her. I'll spend more time with him. I won't nag him anymore, then he'll love me the way I want to be loved. I'll keep the house clean. I'll get a job. I'll be more affectionate.* We can come up with all kinds of "deals" to get people to love us, but bargaining is still not totally objective. The responsibility still remains on us alone, and we are still believing the best about the other person.

Believing the best of others is usually good and right. It is usually a virtue. But when a person has proven by months and years of irresponsible, manipulative behavior that he is pathological, then believing the best is not a virtue. It is naive and foolish. It is the haven of denial.

Bargaining is an expression of hope; hope that the other person will change and give us the love and worth that we need. But it is a false hope. The hard truth, the reality of objective observation, leads us to a painful but honest conclusion: we need to give up. We need to abandon the vain hope that the other person will change and give us what we need. Letting go doesn't sound very spiritual. It doesn't sound very godly, but it is. Letting go is a reflection of reality, and it is an act of abandoning the idol of pleasing others and being accepted and loved by them as the way to win self-worth. Actually, it is an act of worship to the Lord.

When we let go, when we stop bargaining and look the truth in the face, we may become very angry with the one who has lied to us, used us, and hurt us so deeply.

Anger

Anger is a difficult issue to write about. It is, by its nature, volatile and consuming. Many people hold strong but often contrasting opinions about it. Treatments of anger are sometimes superficial, and sometimes complex and confusing. Here's my best shot:

All anger is not wrong, nor is all anger right. Some of it is good and wholesome, but much of it is sin. There is a difference between feeling angry and acting angry. It isn't wrong to feel angry when it is a natural response to some type of pain in our environment. Some people see this anger as sin, and they either deny that it exists or they express it indirectly (passive aggression) and inappropriately.

The active expression of anger can be either righteous or unrighteous. It can either hurt or heal. If the feeling of anger prompts us to stop being manipulated, to be independent of others, and to state our case clearly and calmly instead of withdrawing or attaching, then the response to that feeling is good and healthy. If, however, that feeling of anger prompts revenge and/or withdrawal, then the response is destructive. Two classic passages about anger are Eph. 4:26-27 and James 1:19-20. Paul admonishes us to feel angry, but not to express that anger unrighteously:

> *BE ANGRY, AND yet DO NOT SIN; do not let the sun go down on your anger, and do not give the devil an opportunity."*
>
> Eph. 4:26-27

James warns us not to let our expression of anger hurt others:

> *This you know, my beloved brethren. But let everyone be quick to hear, slow to speak and slow to anger; for the anger of man does not achieve the righteousness of God.*
>
> James 1:19-20

For our purposes, we will differentiate between destructive anger and constructive anger. Destructive anger is based on the desire to harm another person. It consists of outbursts, rage, seething, and revenge. Constructive anger is the result of being harmed by another. Too often, however, we cross over the line in our response, and constructive anger quickly becomes destructive. That's why Paul wrote, *Be angry* (constructive anger), *and yet do not sin* (destructive anger).

Most of us have mixed perceptions about anger. If we have repressed it for a long time, it may surface in embarrassing ways. So we rationalize it. We feel guilty about it. We ignore it. We hate ourselves for it. In general, most of us have consciously or unconsciously come to the conclusion that anger is wrong. In this process of our healing, we may try to skip from anger to grief because grief seems more acceptable. But we won't be able to thoroughly grieve until we have come to grips with the reality of our anger.

Hurting people have difficulty with anger because present offenses are complicated and compounded by a backlog of repressed anger at past offenses. The command *Do not let the sun go down on your anger* has been violated so many times that denial and repression have become the normal way of dealing with anger. The answer is objectivity and honesty about that repressed anger, but we cannot dredge up every offense of the past and deal with them in a day. It takes longer than that! After a period of honest reflection and honest expression of repressed emotions, we are then able to deal effectively with each offense as it occurs, not letting "the sun go down" on our anger.

Perhaps a diagram will help describe how repressed anger makes it difficult to deal effectively with present offenses.

The response to a new offense is complicated and compounded by a backlog of past offenses. Most of us either repress our anger at the new offense, too, or respond in anger that is disproportionate to the offense.

Through being honest about repressed anger and expressing it in a safe environment, the backlog is gradually diminished.

Eventually, our backlog of anger is expressed and dealt with. Because new offenses are not complicated by repressed anger, we can respond more objectively with appropriate anger and forgiveness.

In the unconditional love and acceptance of God, we have an environment in which we can be honest and vulnerable. We not only can acknowledge our present hurt and anger, but we can be objective about the cumulative hurts of the past—and the resulting anger that has been stored inside us. David instructs us to be open and honest with God because He cares for us:

> *Trust in Him at all times, O people; pour out your heart before Him; God is a refuge for us.*
> Ps. 62:8

Many codependents stop their progress at this phase of the process because they have developed an aversion to expressing anger—especially about the one who has offended them the most. Unless this impasse can be broken, they will not proceed to grief, acceptance, and ultimately to stability and health. Here are a few reasons people can't, or won't, be angry.

- They believe: *All anger is wrong and sinful. If I am angry, then I must be a bad person.*
- They believe: *If there is any problem in the relationship, it must be my fault!* They feel a misguided, blind loyalty to the one who has deeply hurt them. This loyalty is coupled with pangs of guilt at even the thought of being angry with him or her.
- They excuse the offense: *Oh, that's okay. I don't mind. It doesn't hurt me. I'm used to it by now, and besides, she couldn't help it.*
- They are afraid of the backlash of anger, rejection, ridicule, withdrawal, and wrath of the other person.
- They are afraid that after experiencing healing, warmth, and intimacy in the relationship, they will be hurt all over again, which is too great a risk.
- Being angry is not an option that they will even consider. Often, seething anger and bitter hurt are repressed. In their denial, codependents won't acknowledge any problem at all.

- In their lack of objectivity, they only see the good things about the other person. They either don't see anything harmful, selfish, or negative, or if they do, they quickly rationalize those characteristics.
- They have been taught by some Bible teachers that their parents or spouse is their authority, and that they must unconditionally submit to them. In a dysfunctional family, this submission is used to manipulate, condemn, and use the codependent.

It is very important to find a safe environment of unconditional love and acceptance to develop honesty about the cumulative effects of repressed anger in your life. Constructive anger occasionally moves to destructive anger. You need someone to give you both affirmation and correction. Exposing hurts and anger can be awkward and difficult, and will take time. However, at the heart of this constructive anger and pain is a sense of stability that is based on objectivity. Even though it can be tremendously painful to express these emotions, you are still likely to experience a sense of satisfaction in knowing why you've struggled so much for so long. After your anger is spent, however, you will likely feel a sense of loss.

Grief

"There is a little girl in me who was never loved by her father," Susan said sadly, "and she never will be."

Will said, "I had such hopes and dreams for our marriage, but now it will never be what I hoped it would be. I feel so empty."

"Our darling little girl was so cute, so loving," Margaret said, as she remembered her daughter. "But drugs have ruined her life...and almost ruined ours, too. We'll just have to make the best of it now."

When the vat of anger has been drained to a trickle, a sense of loss begins to dominate us. We grieve as if someone had died because it seems like someone did—us. We had something and it was taken away. Or we realize that we have wanted something—love and acceptance from a certain person—very badly, but will never have it. We wanted intimacy, warmth, and laughter, but we feel only hurt and emptiness.

Janice was progressing through this process, and she described her grief to me: "I was sitting in church one day and I had the strangest feeling. I felt like I was going to cry and throw up at the same time. I thought, *I'm losing it! I'm really going crazy!* After the service, I realized that I was grieving. I guess that I've bottled up my emotions for so long that they came out in a strange way."

Over the next several months, Janice continued to grieve. She felt sad. She felt lonely. But she also knew that this was a part of the process. She really wasn't going crazy. She was becoming healthy!

How do we grieve? How long do we grieve? Good questions, but there are no clear and simple answers. There are no formulas for grieving. We grieve by giving ourselves the freedom to feel loss for as long as it takes. It helps greatly to have someone to affirm you and give you perspective (Does this sound like a broken record?) as you go through this process. You need someone who will listen to you and comfort you without giving quick and easy solutions to get you to feel better.

Months may go by. Your emotions will vary. Sometimes you will feel the catharsis of the healing process, but sometimes, you will feel very sad. You may become emotional over things that never affected you before—an act of kindness toward you, a crying child, a new offense. All of this is normal and healthy. It is part of being a real person with real feelings in real relationships. The Lord will give you grace and comfort. Then you will be able to accept all that has happened to you.

Acceptance

Finally, we experience a sense of peace and calm. The bargaining, anger, and grief have been exposed and expressed. We are objective about life: its good and bad, its righteousness and wickedness. We are uncomfortable with simple, easy answers knowing that they just don't work. We gain a new depth in our relationship with the Lord and with people. We discover new perspectives on life, new values, and new lifestyles. We don't feel driven to accomplish every goal because we have a new set of priorities. We enjoy a healthy blend of independence from others and a new dependence on the Lord. We can say no, and we can admit being wrong.

People who can see their lives with objectivity can help others be objective, too. There is wisdom in their perceptions, and they can comfort those who hurt because they understand their hurts (2 Cor. 1:3-5).

Mark asked, "When I get to that phase, will I experience total freedom? Will I be completely free from the effects of my codependency, or will I always be scarred?" I thought for a minute, then I told Mark about an incident in my life years ago.

When I was young, our family bought some Roman candles to shoot on New Year's Eve. My father lit them and off they flew into the night, exploding in all kinds of colors. I had been parked under the arm of my mother on the front steps, but lighting the fireworks looked like lots of fun, so after my father lit one, I ran down the steps and grabbed it. I held it straight up, waiting for it to blast up into the sky. Instead, it backfired inside the sleeve of the winter jacket I was wearing!

Like it was yesterday, I vividly remember looking through sheets of tears at my parents. They grabbed me and took me inside to see how badly I was hurt. It was worse than they could have imagined. At the hospital, they learned that I had third-degree burns over most of my forearm.

For the next several months, the burn required almost constant attention. Wrapping, unwrapping, putting on medicine, making trips to the doctor, crying in the night. My exuberant little sprint to grab the firework had resulted in agony for the whole family. After a few months, scar tissue began to form on the burn. Gradually, the burn required less and less attention.

Today, there is still a sizable scar on my arm, but I rarely think about it until I see someone staring at it in the summer when I'm wearing a short-sleeved shirt. Though the scar remains, the pain has been gone for years, and the consuming attention it required is just a memory.

Codependency is a deep wound that requires a lot of attention for a while. Even the emotional bandaging and medication seem to hurt, but if it is well-treated, scar tissue will gradually form as the healing process continues. Though the scar may remain, the pain will gradually be replaced by healing and health. This process isn't pleasant, but it is essential if the wound is to heal.

Taking responsibility

In conjunction with grieving losses, the healing process also involves taking responsibility to make progress and take specific steps toward healing and restoration. A person in the healing process needs to take responsibility to develop perception, experience and express love, and build a healthy sense of separateness based on a positive self-esteem.

Perception—The process of gaining an accurate perception of yourself and your relationships is usually slow, with a few flashes of insight from time to time. Yet after a while, you will develop realistic expectations. You won't expect the process to be over quickly. You won't be as surprised when you see deeper levels of pain or other unhealthy aspects of relationships that have characterized your life. And you will become more comfortable with the complexities of life, not expecting simple answers to explain everything. The primary responsibility of teaching and developing perception lies with the family (Deuteronomy 6:4-12; Proverbs 3:1-4). This brings us to the central point of this chapter.

Dysfunctional families fail, to one degree or another, in a couple of areas: either to impart truth accurately, or more importantly, to develop the mechanisms (belief systems) which enable family members to perceive accurately. When these mechanisms are damaged or undeveloped, truth becomes distorted. Adding more truth won't solve the problem until the underlying mechanisms are developed. The problem then, in dysfunctional families, is not just one of misinformation. The root problem is that the ability to accurately perceive is damaged. A codependent may have learned to "read" others very well (in order to please them), but he doesn't recognize reality in his own life or the motives for his interactions with others.

Love—Most theologians and psychologists agree that the central need in life is the ability to give and receive love. If you have been in a home where people were loved and affirmed, especially if you are from a dysfunctional family and have been in the process of growth for a while, then you probably can appreciate both the need for and the power of love.

In our culture, love has been redefined and reduced to a point that the term usually connotes only a pleasant feeling or sexual attraction. But the biblical description of love is more precise and is explained in three terms.

Eros describes the love of passion, usually between a man and a woman.

Phileo means brotherly affection. It is based on some characteristic of the other person, such as, "I love you because you are pretty (or strong, or smart, or whatever)."

Agape is the term that describes the self-giving, unconditional affection of God (and of God's people). This love recognizes intrinsic value in the other person and continues in spite of his or her performance. It is a commitment to the well-being of another even when it is not pleasant or convenient. Paul described this kind of selfless affection and valuing of others in his first letter to the believers in Corinth:

> *If I speak with the tongues of men and of angels, but do not have love, I have become a noisy gong or a clanging cymbal.*
>
> *And if I have the gift of prophecy, and know all mysteries and all knowledge; and if I have all faith, so as to remove mountains, but do not have love, I am nothing.*
>
> *And if I give all my possessions to feed the poor, and if I deliver my body to be burned, but do not have love, it profits me nothing.*
>
> *Love is patient, love is kind, and is not jealous; love does not brag and is not arrogant,*
>
> *Does not act unbecomingly; it does not seek its own, is not provoked,*

Does not take into account a wrong suffered, does not rejoice in unrighteousness, but rejoices with the truth;
Bears all things, believes all things, hopes all things, endures all things.
Love never fails.

1 Cor. 13:1-8a

The love of God is to be imparted by the family, the body of Christ, the Word of God, and the Holy Spirit. People from dysfunctional families, however, often have difficulty experiencing God's love even when they understand it theologically. The family environment is tremendously important. Feeling valued, accepted, and loved is the first critical stage in our development—the bonding stage.

Dr. Burton White has said that children need "irrational love" to enable them to develop a healthy sense of self-esteem. In dysfunctional families, that sense of being valued is, to some degree, impaired. One lady, who was sexually abused as a child, was plagued by intense feelings of self-hatred. The son of an alcoholic realized that his father told him that he cared, but his actions communicated that he really didn't love his son. A young woman realized that she was appreciated as long as she played the role of "the good child" in her family, but the moment she didn't play that role, her parents and brother condemned her until she meekly complied with their demands.

It is easy to see how someone who doesn't feel loved would be attracted to many codependents. The attentive, compassionate codependent gives the hurting person both the time and affection that he craves. But the person often gives up control and self-respect in the bargain because the codependent isn't satisfied with merely providing time and affection. He also wants to control how the other person thinks, feels, and acts. The relationship looks like love. It often feels like love. But it is clouded by the codependent's desire to control.

Again, people from dysfunctional families think their lives are normal. They may think they are experts on the subject, but to some degree, they don't even know what love feels like. If you are from a dysfunctional family, and/or if you have been in a relationship with a codependent for a long time, you need to find a healthy relationship so you can learn to give and receive love. You won't find any perfect people, but you can find people who are honest with you, who value you as a person, who are patient with you, and who forgive you when you offend them. In that kind of environment, you can learn to enjoy being yourself.

Separateness—The codependent person in your life has certainly been on—or trying to get on—your ranch. He has been trying to make decisions for you and get you to think, feel, and act the way he thinks you should. If you developed a healthy independence prior to this relationship, then you probably have been able to maintain a degree of separateness. You have said "no." You have been honest about your feelings. You have chosen to make your own decisions. If, however, you are from a dysfunctional family and you haven't gone through much of the healing process, then you probably have difficulty with separateness—especially now in your relationship with the codependent in your life.

Charles is from a home where his father is a workaholic and his mother is a codependent. His mother smothered Charles with attention—and control. In most of his relationships, especially dating relationships, Charles looked to other people for cues to know what to think and how to feel. When asked a question, he would reply, "I don't know," unless he was absolutely sure that his answer would be accepted. He finally married a woman just like his mother—someone who would live on his ranch and take care of him.

Betty is from a similar family, but responds quite differently. Instead of quickly giving in, she is tremendously defensive. She told me that she feels very guilty when she doesn't give in, but she is so angry when others try to tell her what to do that she refuses to acquiesce.

Charles hides. Betty has her guns blazing! Both have given up most of their ranches. Two codependents sometimes get into a relationship where each one lives on the other's ranch: rescuing, fixing, controlling, and condemning. Each is trying to satisfy his need for love and value by getting the other person to value him. Their relationship becomes almost a game to see who can control whom. Though there may be times of ecstasy, there is often hurt, confusion and anger. Both desperately want to be loved, but the method used to gain love is to manipulate the other. They both then feel used, not loved. They need the freedom of separateness so they can extend love and let each other make his own decisions.

Separateness, like perception and love, is learned in the context of positive, honest relationships where people talk openly of their hurts, fears, joys, and hopes. If you have been letting others control how you think, feel, and act, or if you feel guilty when you don't let them control you, then you need to get into a relationship with someone who will encourage you to find reality in your life and to help you take the next step. A pastor, counselor, or friend who understands these issues can be of great value to you at this stage.

Elements Which Contribute to the Process

The process of emotional, spiritual, and relational healing is multifaceted. Let's look at some elements of this process:

Right thinking

Repentance means "to change"; to change one's mind, purpose, and actions. It is more than just the experience of sorrow; it is the changing of our attitude and actions when we have realized that they are sinful and dishonoring to God. As an offensive weapon, repentance has two sharp edges. The first allows us to discern and reject false beliefs. When situations occur which trigger certain beliefs that produce ungodly responses, we must:

1. be honest about our emotions;
2. trace the emotions back to their source and identify the false belief(s); and
3. consciously and assertively reject the false belief(s).

The following diagram illustrates this process:

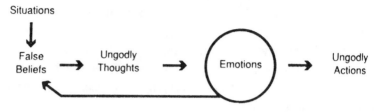

Trace the emotions back to the false beliefs

The second edge of repentance is the replacement of false beliefs with the truth of God's Word. By affirming God's truth about our worth, we will lodge it deep within our hearts and minds, and begin to reshape our thinking, feelings, and behavior. Then, the process of having the truth modeled to us, affirmed in us, taught to us, and applied by us over time will enable us to increasingly experience freedom in different areas of our lives.

The following chart can help you to confront and overcome the false beliefs through the truth of God's Word.

False Belief	God's Specific Solution
I must meet certain standards in order to feel good about myself.	Because of **justification**, I am completely forgiven and fully pleasing to God. I no longer have to fear failure.
I must have approval of certain others to feel good about myself.	Because of **reconciliation**, I am totally accepted by God. I no longer have to fear rejection.
Those who fail are unworthy of love and deserve to be punished.	Because of **propitiation**, I am deeply loved by God. I no longer have to fear punishment or punish others.
I am what I am. I cannot change. I am hopeless.	Because of **regeneration**, I have been made brand new, complete in Christ. I no longer need to experience the pain of shame.

If false beliefs remain in our minds, unchallenged and unrejected, they retain an unconscious influence on our emotions and reactions. Consequently, our warfare is a sustained and continuous battle. Every disturbing situation provides us with an opportunity to discover our incorrect thinking, to reject our world-acquired beliefs, and exchange them for the truth. This is a daily process for every Christian; only this aggressive, conscious, truth-seeking effort can reverse years of habitually wrong thinking.

Affirming God's truth is a weapon of great spiritual value. Through this process, we state God's truth as our own perspective. Continual affirmation gradually produces beliefs which result in correct thinking, which then result in godly responses. Affirming the truths of God's Word enables us to overcome the deception of the enemy (Rev. 12:10). The following diagram illustrates this process:

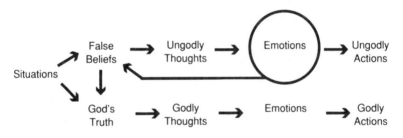

In practice, our actual experience may not be quite so neat and precise. Our emotions, beliefs, and behavior are the product of years of experiences and relationships. They can be very strong, very confusing, and very difficult to understand.

Although the above diagram is a general model, it is helpful in identifying some of the roots of our behavior and emotions, and can serve as an aid to direct us to follow God's truth in our growth process.

A Support System

As the person experiences the new sensation of people asking caring questions instead of demanding his instant rescuing, he will begin to feel valued as a person. As he takes the risk of being honest about his weaknesses and sins, he can experience the forgiveness and acceptance of others (especially yours). As people listen to him without correcting him, he will gain confidence. As others let him make his own decisions, feel his own feelings, and think his own thoughts, he will gain a new sense of strength. As people genuinely care for him, he will learn to experience authentic love. He will begin to believe that God isn't harsh or aloof as he originally thought. He will begin to genuinely experience the tender, strong, consistent love of God for him. And he will then learn to express that love to others.

God's Enablement

The truths we have examined can have tremendous implications on our every goal and relationship, but now we need to understand how to actually implement them in our lives. How can we begin to experience positive change? Jesus answered this question in His last time of intimate instruction with His disciples (John 13-16). He told them that He would soon be put to death, but that they would not be left alone: *And I will ask the Father, and He will give you another Helper, that He may be with you forever* (John 14:16). That Helper is the Holy Spirit, who came some fifty days later to direct and empower the believers at Pentecost. That same Holy Spirit indwells each believer today, and serves as our instructor, counselor, and source of spiritual power as we live for Christ's glory and honor.

Who is the Holy Spirit, and why did He come? The Holy Spirit, the third Person of the Trinity, is God and possesses all the attributes of deity. His primary purpose is to glorify Christ and bring attention to Him. Christ said, *He shall glorify Me; for He shall take of Mine, and shall disclose it to you* (John 16:14). The Holy Spirit is our teacher, and He guides us into the truth of the Scriptures (John 16:13). It is by His power that the love of Christ flows through us and produces spiritual fruit within us (John 7:37-39; 15:1-8). This spiritual fruit is described in many ways in the New Testament, including: intimate friendship with Christ (John 15:14); love for one another (John 15:12); joy and peace in the midst of difficulties (John 14:27; 15:11); steadfastness (Eph. 5:18-21); and evangelism and discipleship (Matt. 28:18-20).

Obviously, this fruit is not always evident in the lives of Christians, but why not? As we all know, the Christian life is not an easy one. It is not simply a self-improvement program. True, we may at times be able to make some changes in our habits through our own discipline and determination, but Christianity is not merely self-effort. The Christian life is a supernatural one in which we draw on Christ as our resource for direction, encouragement, and strength.

Time

If we were computers, solutions to our problems would be produced in microseconds. People, however, don't change that quickly. The agrarian metaphors given in the Scriptures depict seasons of planting, weeding, watering, growth, and harvesting. Farmers don't expect to plant seeds in the morning and harvest their crops that afternoon. Seeds must go through a complete cycle of growth, receiving plenty of attention in the process, before they mature. In this age of instant coffee, microwave dinners, and instant banking, we tend to assume that spiritual, emotional, and relational health will be instantaneous. These unrealistic expectations only cause discouragement and disappointment.

Although this book's primary focus is on the cognitive, or right-thinking, aspect of our spiritual growth, we need to remember that all of these elements are required to produce growth and health. Our growth will be stunted and superficial if we don't give proper emphasis to honesty about our emotions, affirming relationships, right thinking promoted through biblical study and application, the ministry of the Holy Spirit, and time.

Some of us seem to respond to this environment of growth very quickly; others, after a few weeks or months; and still others, never at all. Why the difference? Why are some of us able to apply principles of growth so much more readily than others? The answer is that differing factors will produce a variety of responses from different people. Those who respond quickly may not be as wounded as others, or they may already be in an environment which has prepared them for relatively rapid growth.

Some of us are in situations where one or more elements of growth are in some way missing or lacking. We may be trying to deal with our difficulties alone. We may be depending on a rigid structure of discipline for positive change, instead of blending a healthy combination of our responsibility with the Holy Spirit's enabling power. We may be expecting too much too soon, and may be experiencing disappointment with our slow results. Some of us may, in fact, be ready to quit the growth process entirely.

Those of us who can't seem to get the light turned on have the greatest difficulty in beginning this process. We can't see our problems. We may recognize that something is wrong, but can't pinpoint exactly what. Or, our defense mechanisms of denial may be so strong that we're unable to see any needs in our lives at all.

A young man asked me, "What about people from very stable backgrounds? They don't wrestle with the difficulties you're talking about, do they?"

"All of us have a fallen, sinful nature," I responded. "Because of that, we all wrestle to some degree with the fears of failure and rejection, and with feelings of inadequacy, guilt, and shame. Those from stable, loving families are usually better able to determine what their difficulties are, and be honest about them, than those who are shackled by the defense mechanisms that are often developed in dysfunctional families.

"Those from abusive, manipulative, or neglectful families have far more to overcome than those from a healthier home environment," I explained. "Alcoholism, divorce, sexual abuse, physical abuse, workaholism, drug abuse, and other major family disorders leave deep wounds. Many people from backgrounds like these have suppressed their intense hurt and anger for so long that they are simply out of touch with the reality in their lives. Therefore, just as a broken arm requires more time, attention, and therapy for healing than does a small abrasion, people suffering from deep emotional, spiritual, and relational injuries need more time, attention, love, and encouragement than those with more minor wounds. Though the process for recovery may take longer, enjoying health in these areas is still possible if all the elements of healing are applied over its duration."

Another person asked, "Why doesn't just understanding these issues work? Why isn't knowledge enough to produce change?"

"Man is a relational, physical, emotional, and spiritual being," I said. "We develop and learn and grow best in an environment of honesty, love, and affirmation, where all aspects of our nature are given the encouragement to heal."

A woman asked me, "What do I need to do to begin seeing some results?"

"Put yourself in an environment of growth, which includes all the elements of honesty, affirming relationships, right thinking, the ministry of the Holy Spirit, and time. I can't tell you how or when growth will come—but I know that it will come if you are patient and persistent."

A businessman asked, "Why do I not see much change in my life?" After talking with him for awhile, three issues surfaced which can be common to many of us: First, this gentleman had advanced significantly in his profession by performing well and pleasing people. Although he had received promotions, raises, prestige, and comfort, he still wasn't happy. Yet, it was difficult for him to consider living by a pattern of behavior other than that which had seemingly brought him so far.

In addition, this man was afraid of how he might respond to the generosity of God's love and freedom. He feared that he would either abuse God's grace or be so changed by it that some of his friends and business associates might make fun of him and ultimately reject him.

Finally, he feared that if he did respond wholeheartedly to God's love, the Lord might test his faith by making his life miserable. "I couldn't stand that," he told me. "My life is painful now, but at least I'm used to it. If I surrender completely to God, my life might get totally out of control."

These and many other reasons make the process of spiritual, relational, emotional, and mental health elusive to many people. But again, honesty is our starting point. When we are willing to be open about our thoughts and fears, we generally find that others have thought and felt much the same way.

Our growth toward wholeness and maturity is a journey which won't be completed until we join the Lord in heaven. The Apostle Paul understood this, and saw himself as being in the middle of this process. He wrote to the Philippian believers:

> *Not that I have already obtained it, or have already become perfect, but I press on in order that I may lay hold of that for which I was laid hold of by Christ Jesus.*
> Phil. 3:12

If Paul, the foremost missionary and writer of much of the New Testament, saw himself as being "in the process," we can be encouraged to continue in the process toward change as well. It will help to have reasonable expectations about our progress. Sometimes, we will experience flashes of insight and spurts of growth, but the process of healing and renewal will more often be slow and methodical. Our emotions, too, may occasionally be very pleasant and positive, but when God's light shines on another area of hurt in our lives, we will likely experience another round of pain and anger. Remember that healing can only continue as we put ourselves in an environment characterized by honesty, affirming relationships, right thinking, the Holy Spirit's love and power, and time.

Evaluation Questions

1. What principles from this section seem most helpful to you? Why?

2. What aspects of this section are confusing to you?

3. How will you get these clarified? (Who can you talk to? What books can you read?)

4. What specific points will you apply from this section? How will you apply these?

8

GETTING A HANDLE ON THE PROCESS

Objectives:
- to understand how to handle specific events in the healing process; and
- to get a clearer grasp of the individual's responsibility for his decisions and his role in relationships.

The previous chapter outlines the overall process of emotional, spiritual, and relational healing. In this chapter, we will examine specific events within that process.

Virtually every event in our lives is colored to some degree by our past. As we learn to grieve our losses (of dignity, love, self-esteem, hope, value, etc.) and take responsibility, we also need to learn specific skills. We can learn to *identify* our thoughts, feelings, and behavior; *detach* to gain objectivity, and *decide* to take action which is positive and healthy.

As you lead your group, be sure to help them learn these skills. Let's look at these three elements.

Identify

Identifying dysfunctional behavior may seem like a very cognitive exercise, but it usually elicits a flood of emotions as we realize how deeply we have been affected. There is both good and bad news in this realization. The good news is: there is hope! The Lord can give us wisdom and strength, and a friend can give us the encouragement we need to fight our battles. The bad news is: what you see is probably only the first layer of the onion. As you deal with the hurts, fears, anger, and habits, there is yet another layer that will be exposed. Is that discouraging to you? It probably is, but this is reality, and we need to face reality no matter how difficult it is. To help you and others identify dysfunctional behavior, refer to "Characteristics of Individuals from Dysfunctional Families" in Chapter Six of this manual (pages 117-120).

A person's progress in the healing process largely depends upon his ability to increasingly identify reality: his family background, relationships, control, manipulation, hurt, anger, feelings, thoughts, and behaviors.

Two psychologists, Joseph Luft and Harry Ingram, developed a model which describes how much we know and disclose about ourselves. This model is called Johari's Window (The name is a combination of the psychologists' first names.) and it identifies four areas in relationships: the shared area, the blind area, the hidden area, and the unknown area.

	Known to self	Not known to self
Known to others	1 Shared area	3 Blind area
Not known to others	2 Hidden area	4 Unknown area

The goal of the group is to help each member enlarge his "Shared area" through developing trust and providing feedback using good communication skills.

	Known to self	Not known to self
Known to others	1 Shared area.	3 Blind area
Not known to others	2 Hidden area	4 Unknown area

The "Shared area" represents what a person knows about himself and has willingly shared with one or more others. Secrets are kept in the "Hidden area" which represents that which the individual knows about himself but does not disclose openly. Conversely, the "Blind area" indicates information which the individual does not know about himself but others do. Finally, the "Unknown area" is known only to God.

A major goal of the group process is to facilitate growth of the "Shared area." To do so, the individual must risk disclosures of himself. Trust, confidentiality, respect, and the ministry of the Holy Spirit encourage such self-disclosure.

To reduce the "Hidden area," the member may have to deal with shame. He will have to take the risks of painful self-disclosure and the possible rejection of others in the group. Scripture encourages disclosure of faults, and disclosure often results in God's forgiveness and healing (James 5:16).

Reduction of the "Blind area" requires members to risk providing honest feedback. Skills are needed. The individual must be lovingly told of his faults that others have observed. He must learn to be objective.

Positive reinforcement is essential to each members' progress. In *The Search for Significance*, Robert McGee directs readers to develop a list of Biblical aspects of self-esteem. People can reflect on these several times daily. This list includes:

I am loved;
I am accepted;
I am pleasing to God;
I am forgiven; and
I am complete because of Christ's redemption.

It will help a member to listen more objectively if he has affirmation from the group. Confrontational feedback describes specific behaviors, attitudes, and discrepancies as well as affirmation about progress and growth. Proverbs says that a wise man will change his ways when confronted. A fool will never turn from his folly (Prov. 9:8-9; 16:22-23).

Finally, reduction of the "Unknown area" requires the ministry of the Holy Spirit. It is a wonderful experience to have the Holy Spirit bring up an area in your life. As you interact with God, He will reveal areas to you that you need to address. Paul tells us that God has only one motive for discipline—love. The result of godly discipline is for our personal growth and character. God never disciplines us because He is tired of us or fed up with our behavior.

Detach

Detachment requires time, objectivity, and distance (emotionally, physically, or both). Circumstances vary so widely that there cannot be a formula for detaching, but there is a question that can help you: *What do I need* (time, space, objectivity) *so that I can reflect on this situation?*

Some Perspectives on Detaching

Charting a new course for a specific situation or for a lifetime can be very awkward and frightening. There are so many changes, so many emotions, and seemingly, so little time. These are some perspectives on the process of detaching:

Detaching in love or anger

It is best to detach calmly and with a loving attitude, but that isn't always possible. It may seem harsh or selfish to put such a premium on detachment, but being controlled by someone and pleasing him above all else is not a good thing. It is idolatry. If you have the choice either to detach in anger or in love, try to do it in love. But by all means, *detach.* Melody Beattie wrote:

> *I think it is better to do everything in an attitude of love. However, for a variety of reasons, we can't always do that. If you can't detach in love, it's my opinion that it is better to detach in anger rather to stay attached. If we are detached, we are in a better position to work on (or through) our resentful emotions. If we're attached, we probably won't do anything other than stay upset.* *

Anger can actually be used constructively in the process of detaching. It is a strong motivation to develop your independence and identity. Constructive anger can be seen in thoughts like: *I refuse to be manipulated again,* or *I'm not going to take this anymore; I'm going to detach so I can develop my own identity and make my own decisions.*

Detaching perfectly

Some of us are such obsessive–compulsive perfectionists that we think we have to do everything perfectly when we detach! One woman told me that she was afraid to detach because she "might not do it just right, and what would my father say if I made a mistake?" After a few minutes, she realized that this perfectionism and fear were the very reasons she needed to detach!

A young man who was learning to detach came to a startling realization. He was driven to succeed and to always "be right," but one day, as he sat in a sales meeting, the thought hit him, I *don't*

---

* Melody Beattie, *Codependent No More* (New York: Hazelden Foundation, 1987), p. 58.

have to be right. He did not instantly become irresponsible, but instead, became more bold and confident as he developed the habit of detaching.

If we believe that we have to say and do everything perfectly when we detach, then we are still carrying an oppressive weight of responsibility. Be realistic. Detaching requires a major change in thoughts, feelings, and emotions. Changes like these are not computerized. We are not robots. We are people, and people need time, practice, and patience to change deeply ingrained habits.

How would a "normal" person respond?

Drawing a comparison between our unhealthy reactions and the healthy responses of a "normal" person is very instructive. Some of us, however, may recoil at this thought because our perception is that dysfunctional or codependent people are giving and loving and that "normal" people are selfish and prideful. That perception demonstrates a continued lack of objectivity. It still sees the virtue in rescuing without seeing its hidden selfishness and idolatry.

It is true that "normal" people, like all of us, are sinners who are prone to selfishness and pride, but for our purposes we are using normal to mean simply healthy and independent. A healthy, independent person may seem terribly selfish because he isn't controlled by the whims of others, but we don't need to label him as a terrible, awful, no good, very bad person because he makes his own decisions.

Expect conflict

When you stop playing an unhealthy role in your family, don't expect everybody to applaud you for your growth and development! They have lived their lives by having you rescue them as they controlled you. As they realize that you are no longer controllable, they may step up the pressure. They may use stronger manipulation: more guilt, more condemnation, and more withdrawal. They may be accusing: "You are so selfish!"

When you stop playing your unhealthy role in the family, expect conflict; expect to be isolated from the family. As the family re-forms its boundaries, family members may leave you on the outside.

The fear of this isolation is the motivation that often compels dysfunctional or codependent people to continue to be used, neglected, and controlled. It takes both objectivity and courage to take these bold and necessary steps.

Freedom, confusion, and pain

In our era of advanced technology, change comes with the push of a button. But people aren't machines. We don't make major changes quickly and effortlessly. The process of identifying, detaching, and deciding produces a hodge-podge of conflicting emotions and thoughts. Like being cut free from the ocean liner that is going in the wrong direction, we have a new sense of freedom and independence. But with that freedom comes the pain of realizing how dysfunctional behavior has damaged our lives and the confusion of not being confident and secure in our new direction.

Don't despair if you feel awkward and afraid as you learn to detach. These feelings are simply a part of the reality of change. Accept them for now. They will gradually abate as your confidence grows. You will increasingly enjoy your independence and freedom.

Is divorce a good option?

For some, the pain and bitterness of their marriage makes divorce seem to be a viable, attractive form of detachment. There are some counselors who recommend divorce as a way to ease the pain and escape from a seemingly incorrigible relationship, but this may not be the answer. A temporary separation may be in order to allow the partners to detach, to get good counseling, and to develop biblical convictions about marriage. Too often, a hurting person will dump one spouse only to find another to control and rescue, and the cycle continues.

This is a sticky, emotion-charged issue. There are many views that are strongly held. The scope of this book doesn't include an adequate treatment of divorce, separation, and remarriage, but you may want to read *Jesus and Divorce*, by Bill Heth and Gordon Wenham, or *Love Must Be Tough*, by James Dobson. Before you make any major decisions about divorce, consult a competent, qualified Christian counselor or pastor.

How can you tell if you are detached?

It would be ludicrous to say that you haven't detached until you are perfectly calm and loving in your attitudes. With detachment often comes a range of emotions which, in the early stages, are often quite confusing. Nonetheless, you can tell that you are detaching if you have removed yourself from situations to feel and think, if there is a growing objectivity about the contrast between dysfunctional reactions and healthy responses, and if you are experiencing a growing sense of independence.

When you can identify your feelings and behaviors, and then think clearly and objectively about them, you are detaching. Recognize your guilt, fear, rescuing, and controlling tendencies, and realize that these are pathological. Don't dabble with them. Aggressively replace them with objectivity and godly choices. Then you will be detaching.

Become attached to the Lord

Detaching involves change: changing our perceptions, our values, our relationships, our view of ourselves, and our view of others. Being dependent upon the approval of others is changed to independence from others, but it also involves a growing dependence on the Lord. As we detach from others, we can become attached to the Lord and deepen our relationship with Him because He is all we have longed for. He is loving and kind, strong and wise. He is not condemning, aloof, and manipulative. He can be trusted.

The affirmation and objectivity of a consistent friend

Detaching is difficult. It is almost impossible to do alone. You need a friend to help you be objective, to encourage you, and to model a healthy lifestyle. A true friend won't change the way he feels and acts toward you as you go through this difficult process. He will encourage you.

Develop habits of detaching

Don't be too discouraged if your first attempts at detaching are painful and awkward. Drastic change takes time, patience, practice, and courage. The more you try to detach, the more confident you will become, and eventually, it will become a very constructive habit for you.

Decide

It is possible to detach, to feel, to think, and to consider your options, but then to be immobilized and not make any decision at all. After we have reflected, we need the courage to act in positive, healthy ways. We need to stop rescuing and controlling, and start saying and doing those things that reflect independence, security, strength, and health. This is extremely important, both for our own sake and for the sake of those we typically rescue and control.

Responding in a Healthy, Realistic Way*

Your relationship with that particular person you care for has probably been characterized by some combination of rescuing, outbursts of anger, displaced anger, compliance, withdrawal, guilt, hurt, loneliness, pity for him, and pity for yourself. A sense of loyalty has probably contributed to your inability to see the relationship objectively. You may have thought that any negative thoughts or emotions (even though you've had many of them) are signs that there is something dreadfully wrong—with you!

Now you are growing in your objectivity. You are learning that you've repressed emotions that you didn't even know existed. This is difficult, but you're getting in touch with your feelings. Your source of security is changing. You're learning to make your own decisions. All of these are good things, but there's that person: your spouse, your sibling, your parent, your child, your classmate, who has hurt you deeply. What do you do? What do you say?

Remember to identify, detach, and decide. Recognize how you feel and how you act when you see or think of that person. Then detach so you have the time and space necessary to think and feel. You may be able to detach calmly, but you may not. Even if you

---

* This section is excerpted from *Codependency* [Rapha Publishing/Word, Inc.,] and is written for someone who is in the healing process. The principles, however, apply broadly to anyone in the process, not codependents only.

have to detach in anger, remember that not detaching is prolonging idolatry. So, detach. Ask yourself questions so you will see what is really going on. Then make your own choices about what to say and do.

Set limits. Decide what you can live with for right now. Decide on the extent of your communication and contact with that person. Determine which issues you will discuss and which ones you won't. If you decide on these ahead of time, you will be much less likely to succumb to the pressure of the moment and give in to manipulation or condemnation. The relationship has been on his terms for perhaps your whole life, but it can be on your terms now. This isn't selfish. Remember, you're the one who is trying to live in reality, not the other person. It is perfectly good and right to insist on making your own decisions based on reality. Too often, we have believed lies, lived by deception, and made our decisions to rescue and feel guilty based on a world of unreality. This can now end. Base your life on what is really real, not on what a dysfunctional person believes and says is real.

How much do you say? Do you tell that person all about codependency and how messed up you've been because of your relationship with him? Do you describe your dark thoughts, your bitterness, hatred, and fear? The principle here is: express yourself fully to God, and express yourself appropriately to the other person. As you recall, David encouraged us to: "Trust in Him at all times...Pour out your heart before Him" (Ps. 62:8), but we are not to pour out our hearts to people. Only a fool delights in telling everything he knows: "A fool does not delight in understanding, but only in revealing his own mind" (Prov. 18:2). The question is not: *How much can I blast him?* but rather, *What will help that person? How much does he need to know at this time and this place?*

You may tell that person a lot or very little. As your response to him changes, he may ask you what's going on. But he may not. As you consider what to do in this relationship, seek the advice of a mature, godly, knowledgeable person to give you perception and encouragement.

Don't expect to do all of this perfectly (you perfectionist, you!). Give yourself a break! All of this is new. Because this is such a contrast to how you have related in the past, you can expect to have all kinds of conflicting thoughts and emotions.

And don't expect the other person to say, "Well, now I completely understand. Thank you so much for saying all of this. I'll change today and never treat you that way again." He may say he'll change, but that's what he's said a hundred times before. He may weep and try to elicit your pity. He may withdraw from you. He may say, "Let's talk about this," but he probably doesn't really want to understand your point of view. He probably wants to convince you that you are wrong (poor, misguided, confused person that you are) so that you will return to being the docile, compliant puppet you've always been.

Or he may say, "It's all your fault." The denial of personal responsibility is a common characteristic in manipulative, condemning people. Scott Peck described such people in his book, *People of the Lie*. He wrote that they do not recognize their "dark side," that propensity to evil that all of us have. They are so steeped in denial that they cannot even see how they manipulate and condemn others. They may say, "I'm sorry," but what they mean is, *I'm sorry you feel that way. I've never done anything wrong, but you have!* They want quick, superficial forgiveness so the relationship can go back to its pathological status quo.

When we detach from that "other person," it is usually awkward. Karen said, "I can't even pray for him anymore. I feel so strange. I know what I'm doing is right, but shouldn't I be able to pray for him?" She was feeling guilty and confused. Her friend helped her to understand the situation more clearly. Her friend told her, "That's okay, Karen. God can take care of him without your prayers. He wants you to concentrate on detaching and getting your security from Him for now. Later, you can start praying for him again." Your life is changing, so expect a variety of changes in your thoughts and emotions. It's all a part of the process.

Realistic expectations are vital to your relationship. He or she may change, but it is foolish to expect resolution and reconciliation very soon, if ever. Let your identity in Christ and His lordship fill your thoughts, not dreams of intimacy with "that person." He or she may never change, but you can. You can be unhooked. You can be independent, healthy, and realistic.

Excusing or Forgiving

Many of us have been quick to excuse people for how they have hurt us. Excusing, though, is not forgiving. Forgiveness acknowledges the reality of the offense, the full weight of the wrong, and the consequences of the wrong. It then chooses to not hold that offense against the person. When Christ died on the cross, His blood was the payment for our sins so we could be truly forgiven, not just excused for our sins. Our forgiveness of others can mirror the depth of that forgiveness. Paul wrote:

> *Let all bitterness and wrath and anger and clamor and slander be put away from you, along with all malice. And be kind to one another, tender-hearted, forgiving each other, just as God in Christ also has forgiven you.*
> Eph. 4:31-32

Forgiveness does not imply that you have to trust the one you have forgiven. Some of us link the two. We believe, *If I can't trust him, then I haven't really forgiven him.* That belief, however, is not true, and it causes undue pressure and guilt. If a person has proven over the course of months or years that he is untrustworthy, then he can be forgiven, but he should not be trusted. Trusting a proven liar is foolishness, not godliness.

Similarly, understanding is not the same as forgiving. Understanding the painful background of those who have hurt us is often a helpful perception, but most of us respond in pity, excusing harmful behavior and feeling guilty for being angry. In that case, we have understood, but we haven't forgiven.

Beth had been married to Timothy for four years. Timothy was a compulsive workaholic who spent eighty hours a week at the office, and thought about work-related problems when he was at home. Beth had put up with it for a long time, even encouraging him because he was doing so well in his position. But after four years, enough was enough. At the time that Beth was becoming exasperated with Timothy's work habits and neglect of his family, the couple visited his parents at Christmas. On previous visits, Beth had noticed how Timothy's father seemed to be busy most of the time with projects around the house. He had built them a dresser when they were married and several other things as the years had gone by.

Beth now looked at her father-in-law with a more jaundiced eye. *He is a workaholic, too. That's why Timothy is the way he is! No wonder he works so hard. That's all he has ever seen in his father. And Timothy's father neglects his wife the same way Timothy neglects me.* That flash of insight helped put a lot of pieces together for Beth. She felt better. She understood.

As the months went by after their visit with Timothy's parents, Beth tried to excuse Timothy's neglect and preoccupation with his work. Soon, however, she realized that excusing him wasn't the same as forgiving him. She had begun to pity Timothy instead of loving him, but his behavior was wrong. It hurt. Instead of continuing to pity and excuse him, Beth forgave Timothy and committed herself to loving him unconditionally. That meant loving him enough to confront him with the reality of his workaholism and its effects on both of them.

Timothy didn't respond very well. He was angry and defensive, but he agreed to read a book and talk to their pastor about their relationship. After a while, Timothy began to recognize his addiction to success and performance. Together, he and Beth began to experience healing and intimacy in their relationship. It started with reality, forgiveness, unconditional love, and courage.

When a person first learns about codependency or some other dysfunctional behavior, there is a tendency for his view of the one who hurt him and manipulated him to flip-flop from white (he can do no wrong) to black (he can do no right). The anger generated by the realization of hurts, offenses, and damage is a motivation to detach, to stop the idolatry of the relationship, and to begin to establish a new, secure identity. As time goes by, however, greater objectivity will color in shades of gray where black has been before, and the codependent will be able to see the person who has hurt him more clearly. Anger will turn to grief, and grief to acceptance and health. Then he will be able to see both the good and the bad in that person.

He may continue to be manipulated and condemned. His relationship may still be void of trust and intimacy, but he will have confidence that he is living in reality with no grudges. No, it's not a fairy tale ending, but it is good and right and acceptable.

The following is a summary to help you—or the members of your group—develop the habit of putting "handles" on the healing process.

Summary

In this section we will examine a process that you can use to help you take steps toward emotional and relational health.

Identify
Goal: Tell what happened. Describe your feelings and the situation.
Present situation: Identify yourself in the story and tell what role you played.
- Identify the feelings you were having. (Try to detect anger, fear, hurt, or guilt.)

Past situations: Identify similar situations from your past and the role you played in them.
- Have you been feeling the same feelings each time?

Detach
Goal: Realize what is really happening, not only on the outside but on the inside.
Reflect on your...
- **feelings.** Here's how I *really* feel about how I've been acting or how I've been treated.
- **thoughts.** These are the thoughts I am having.
- **actions.** Here's how I *usually* act in this situation.

Reflect on your options.

Aids for Detaching

As you learn to detach so that you can be honest about your feelings and objective about your circumstances, you will see a sharpening contrast between unhealthy and healthy thoughts, feelings, and actions. Perhaps it would be helpful to list some questions to ask yourself when you detach. These are some suggestions.

- *Why did he (she) say (do) that to me?*
- *What did he (she) mean?*
- *How do I feel about it?*
- *How would a healthy person feel?*
- *Is he (she) controlling me? Condemning me? Neglecting me?*
- *Why do I feel guilty? Driven? Afraid? Lonely?*
- *Am I rescuing?*
- *Am I acting as a savior? A Judas?*

Also, it might be helpful to develop some statements that trigger certain thought processes in your mind. This may seem "hokey," but getting a handle on objectivity can be very difficult. Use whatever helps you! Here are a few statements that may help you think and feel.

- *I'm not responsible for making him (her) happy.*
- *I'm not responsible for fixing the problem.*
- *He (she) needs to be responsible for himself (herself).*
- *I can respond calmly.*
- *I can say no.*
- *I can say yes.*
- *I can make my own decisions.*
- *I feel angry, lonely, guilty, driven, afraid.*
- *I am loved, forgiven, and accepted by God through Jesus Christ.*

These statements are about "letting go." On the following page is an explanation of what it means to "let go." You may want to copy this for the people in your group.

"LET GO"

to "let go" does not mean to stop caring;
it means I can't do it for someone else

to "let go" is not to cut myself off;
it's the realization that I can't control another

to "let go" is not to enable,
but to allow learning from natural consequences

to "let go" is to admit powerlessness—which means
the outcome is not in my hands

to "let go" is not to try to change or blame another;
it's to make the most of myself

to "let go" is not to "care for," but to "care about"

to "let go" is not to judge, but to allow another to be a human being

to "let go" is to not be in the middle, arranging all the outcomes,
but to allow others to affect their own destinies

to "let go" is not to be protective;
it's to permit another to face reality

to "let go" is not to deny, but to accept

to "let go" is not to nag, scold or argue, but instead to
search out my own shortcomings and correct them

to "let go" is not to adjust everything to my desires,
but to take each day as it comes, and cherish myself in it

to "let go" is not to criticize and regulate anybody,
but to try to become what I dream I can be

to "let go" is to not regret the past, but to grow and live for the
future

to "let go" is to fear less and love more

Decide

Goal: Make a choice between appropriate and inappropriate behavior.
Choose to act instead of react.
Begin to feel that you are gaining control of yourself.
Choose to repeat your appropriate behavior.
Repeat your new behavior often and reinforce your new feelings.

The following statements and questions will help people make good decisions.

- This is what I will do. This is what I won't do.
- I will not take this kind of behavior anymore.
- I'm not responsible for his (her) happiness.
- I refuse to be manipulated.
- I'm sorry; I wish I could help you, but I can't.
- Why did you say that to me? Do you know how I feel when you say things like that?
- I don't want to talk about this.
- I want to talk about this.

Evaluation Questions

1. What principles from this section seem most helpful to you? Why?

2. What aspects of this section are confusing to you?

3. How will you get these clarified? (Who can you talk to? What books can you read?)

4. What specific points will you apply from this section? How will you apply these?

APPENDIX

QUESTIONS GROUP
LEADERS ASK

Strange and wonderful things can happen when you lead a group! When "the lights come on" in people's lives, leading or facilitating a small group is a very rewarding experience, but sometimes leading others brings confusion and discouragement. Though we cannot possibly cover all of the possible scenarios in this chapter, we will examine at least a few common problems and give some practical suggestions.

What do you do when . . .?

. . . you don't have confidence in your ability to lead a group

Very few people who lead a group for the first time feel comfortable and confident. Usually, the anticipation produces the fear of failure and rejection. If you feel nervous, don't despair. You're normal! Three things will help you develop confidence: preparation, experience, and prayer.

Preparation can raise your confidence level. As you prepare to lead your group, be sure to plan for spontaneous interaction. That may sound like an oxymoron, but relaxed fellowship time will help people develop relationships, and thereby accomplish one of the biggest needs in people's lives, affirmation. Also, work on asking a few good questions. Review the material on pages 28-29 about asking good questions. Don't overload your group with content, and end on time. Preparation doesn't mean that you cram in all the content you can. Remember that context is only one part of the group experience, and plan the interaction and fellowship adequately, too.

Nothing builds confidence like experience. Veteran group leaders have learned from many successes and failures. They fine-tuned their skills by leading many groups in many situations. Have realistic expectations of your leadership. The more groups you lead, the more confident you will become.

One more thing: don't forget to pray. We may do the preparation, planning, and leading, but ultimately it is up to God to change lives. As Paul reminded the believers in Corinth:

> *I planted, Apollos watered, but God was causing the growth.*
> *So then neither the one who plants nor the one who waters is anything, but God who causes the growth.*
> 1 Cor. 3:6-7

. . . your pastor or small group coordinator says you're not ready to lead a group

Some of us may want to lead a group, but we may not be ready yet. Perhaps we haven't acquired the necessary skills; perhaps a tainted reputation prevents our assuming leadership; or perhaps we have not progressed far enough in our own healing process yet. Having someone tell us we aren't ready hurts, but it may save us from far deeper hurts of failing to lead well. Use the next several months or years to focus on the Lord and your own progress. As you grow, the Lord will use you in individuals' lives. After a while, you may be ready to participate in a team which is leading a group. Leadership is a privilege, not a right. Be patient with yourself, and with your pastor or coordinator (see page 8 for group leader qualifications).

. . . your pastor isn't committed to having support groups in his church

Some pastors have had very negative experiences with support groups. Perhaps your pastor has had groups which caused division or attacked his leadership. Be patient with him. Listen to him. Share your desire to serve both him and the church by leading a group, and communicate your loyalty to the church. You may want to show him the Christ-centered books or training materials so he will understand that you are not going to lead a New Age-type group. You may ask him to meet with a Rapha representative or a small group coordinator from another church. Give him time to process this new information and then meet with him again. You may even ask him to sit in on the first group meeting.

. . . you have trouble getting started

Some of us have a difficult time overcoming initial inertia. Perhaps the fear of failure keeps us from doing the detail work of making announcements in Sunday school classes, putting announcements in the bulletin, calling prospective group members, setting the date for the first meeting, and getting started. If you are having trouble getting started, realize that the fear of failure is a common phenomenon. Talk to your small group coordinator. You may want someone to team-lead with you and share the responsibility.

Other factors which may inhibit the start of a group can include the time of the year (the period between Thanksgiving and Christmas is a very difficult time to start a group), lack of support from the church, poor timing of ads, and other logistical problems. Learn from difficulties and plan ahead as much as possible. But don't give up (see pages 8-10 on getting started).

. . . your group dwindles to two or three people

Some of us have unrealistic expectations about the dynamics of groups. We invite four or five people, expecting *each* of them to attend the first meeting—as well as continuing to participate in our group until the Rapture! Experienced group leaders have a different perception. They realize that you usually have to personally invite 25 people for 15 to say they will attend. Of those 15, usually only eight to ten people will actually show up, and of those, only five to seven will be regular attenders after a month or so.

Other factors can cause groups to dwindle, too. Lack of child care, unresolved conflict in the group, holiday seasons, and poor preparation by the leader are some of these. Talk to your small group coordinator or Rapha representative to get some insight and practical suggestions to help your group grow to a healthy size. Remember, quality usually produces quantity (see page 29 on setting the stage).

. . . your group becomes too large

When people find a supportive, nurturing environment and they are able to experience genuine healing, they usually invite their friends to join them. Outreach is a major emphasis of small groups. New members of a group are usually welcome in the first few weeks and some types of groups welcome new members throughout the course of the group. Other groups (such as sexual abuse groups), however, require such a high level of trust that it is very difficult to assimilate new members after the group has established open communication. After that point, the presence of new members may cause the group to regress, so be sure the new person can be trusted. When your group becomes too large, consider developing a new leader within the group and splitting into two groups. When new people want to join at inopportune times, ask them to wait until a new group is started (see page 33 on the size of your group).

. . . people don't seem to be making progress

Virtually every group has people across the spectrum in their response to the material. Some seem to "click" and they grow rapidly. Others don't seem to catch on at all. Most are in between these extremes. Several factors prevent progress in people's lives, including:

- they may be afraid of being overwhelmed by all their repressed emotions;
- their denial may be so strong, they simply can't see reality yet;

- they don't trust the group members; or
- the material doesn't meet their needs.

Take some time to talk with these people individually and privately if they don't seem to be making progress after several weeks or months. Perhaps you'll find that they are actually learning more than you perceived. Perhaps you can help them determine the nature of their problems and help them take some steps. Remember that it is not your responsibility to make them grow. That is up to the Lord and them. Your responsibility is to provide a positive environment for that growth (see page 46 on the elements of an effective small group environment).

... there is interpersonal tension or conflict

Unresolved open conflict can kill a group—not just for that meeting, but completely. Similarly, unspoken tension saps the life from a group. Fellowship is one of the most important aspects of any group, but fellowship isn't just coffee and doughnuts. It is true Christian love: forgiveness, encouragement, correction, and caring. That kind of environment takes time to develop, but it is more powerful than any content. It is life changing!

If conflict is openly expressed in the group, it is appropriate to resolve it openly. Use "I" words, and instruct others to use "I" words, too. If the conflict is between two members and is not brought out openly in the group, go to each one individually and then to both of them together to promote understanding, forgiveness, and reconciliation (see Matt. 18:15-17 and Gal. 6:1-2; also, see pages 37, 60-61 for more on dealing with conflicts).

... members of your group become dependent on one another or get involved with each other sexually

Support groups stimulate open communication of hurts and comfort of those wounds. Many people have never felt that kind of comfort and love before, and they are drawn to each other. Many leaders recommend that the group talk openly about their needs for affection and also, the necessity of setting boundaries on those needs. If you notice that two members are becoming too dependent on each others' affections or if you suspect sexual involvement, go to each of these people individually to share your concerns and listen.

Some group leaders jump too quickly to accuse people of interpersonal dependency or sexual involvement, but most group leaders err on the side of avoiding the conflict that can ensue from these discussions. Pray, talk to your small group coordinator or pastor, and go in love. Perhaps you misunderstood their communications, but perhaps your confronting them will save them years of heartache over poor decisions they are in the process of making now (see page 31 on outside contact).

... someone is unusually quiet in the group

To stimulate the involvement of quiet people, ask them non-threatening questions. You may ask them to tell facts about themselves: where they are from, their hobbies, what they do at home or at work, etc. After they communicate, move on to someone else. Don't make a big deal of their comments. After the meeting, you may want to talk privately with the quiet person, saying that you value his or her input in the group. At that point, the person may express fears of rejection and open the door for meaningful and cathartic communication between the two of you (also see pages 37, and 63-65).

... someone won't stop talking

People who dominate a group by continuous talking can greatly hinder the spirit and progress of the group. Some techniques to divert the conversation from this person include:

- avoiding eye contact with him when he is talking;
- sitting next to him;
- interrupting when there is a pause in his speech—even a brief pause—and asking someone else's opinion; and
- talking to him after the meeting. Communicate that you value his opinions, but that the goal of the group is for everyone to participate equally.

If trouble persists, tell the person that you will have to ask him not to come anymore if he cannot control his compulsion to talk. The good of the group takes precedence over one person's desire to be heard (see page 35 on managing difficulties).

... someone is overwhelmed by anger, hurt, or fear

In the loving environment of support groups, repressed emotions often surface. People feel the long-festered hurts, anger, and fears of years of abuse and neglect, and sometimes these feelings are overwhelming. They may become violently angry, depressed, or unable to function in normal daily activities. Be sure to communicate the possibility of this phenomenon to your group members so they won't be caught off guard if it happens to them. When people are overwhelmed and need additional time, be sure to call your small group coordinator, local Rapha representative, or Rapha's national number (800/383-HOPE) to receive assistance and direction for the hurting person (see pages 40-42, 127 on when to refer).

... someone gets very angry with you

Quite often, a person in the healing process transfers his thoughts and feelings for someone else (typically a spouse or parent) to the person trying to help him. The helping person or counselor in some way represents the father, mother, sibling, or some other person important to the one being helped. Such representation, called *transference*, can be positive. For instance, a person may say to the helper, "You understand me better than my father ever did!" But sometimes this kind of representation is negative.

I once counseled a man who ascribed to me the characteristics of his neglectful father. He became quite angry with me and accused me of not caring for him. While helping another person through the healing process, it is important to expect this kind of behavior. If I hadn't been aware that anger is a common response in these situations, I might have begun to treat him the way his father treated him!

This kind of response by a helper or counselor to the person's attitude toward him is called *counter-transference*. Sometimes the helper may get caught up in the appreciation expressed by the one he is helping. Other times, he may become angry because the person isn't as responsive as the helper feels he should be. In either case, the helper or counselor has lost some objectivity in the relationship.

Transference on the part of a group member is normal. It allows the person to feel previously repressed emotions and verbalize hidden fears, hurt, and anger. But if the helper is unexpectedly blind-sided by another's transference, he can react very negatively, short-circuit the process, and damage the relationship (see page 34 on co-leading and pages 37, 60-61 for more on dealing with conflicts).

. . . the group becomes ingrown

When people experience warmth and affirmation for the first time, they sometimes become protective of these relationships. When the group becomes ingrown, it loses one of its purposes—outreach. One way of keeping the balance of fellowship and outreach is to always have an empty chair in the group, symbolizing the group's commitment to reach out to new people who might fill that chair the next week. Other ways of emphasizing outreach include:

- having a pot-luck dinner and asking members to invite a friend who may want to join the group;
- praying for people—specifically or generally—who need the environment of a support group;
- talking monthly about the balance of fellowship, content, and outreach; and
- being an example to others: when a new person comes to the group, take the initiative to welcome him and get to know him.

(See page 33 for a discussion of open and closed groups and page 62 on the pitfalls of the working stage of a small group.)